Jill's Leading Ladies

The Story of Jill's Six Guide Dogs

Jill's Leading Ladies

The Story of Jill's Six Guide Dogs

Devon Libraries

Jill Allen-King OBE

Foreword by Ann Frye OBE

APEX PUBLISHING LTD

Hardback first published in 2012 by

Apex Publishing Ltd

PO Box 7086, Clacton on Sea, Essex, CO15 5WN, England

www.apexpublishing.co.uk

British Library Cataloguing-in-Publication Data
A catalogue record for this book
is available from the British Library

ISBN HARDBACK: 1-908582-63-4   978-1-908582-63-8

Typeset in 10.5pt Arial

Cover Design: Chris Cowlin

Printed and bound in Great Britain by
MPG Biddles Ltd., King's Lynn, Norfolk

CONTENTS

ACKNOWLEDGMENTS

I should like to thank Peter Wilkins for helping me with the corrections when writing this book. I wrote it myself on my talking computer.

My thanks to my daughter Jacqueline, my husband Alvin, my friends Moira, Barbara and Sue for selecting the photographs. Also to Lynton Sharp for taking the front cover photograph.

PROLOGUE

It is 11 November 2010, just one year since I finished writing my autobiography, Just Jill, which was published on 16 July 2010, and I am on holiday in Majorca with my husband Alvin and my sixth guide dog, Amanda. It is 39 years today since I qualified with my first guide dog, Topsy. Like Amanda, she was a black Labrador, and she gave me back my independence after going totally blind in 1964. Today is Remembrance Day, and 11 November certainly holds many memories for me. It was the date of the birthday of the grandmother I never knew.

HOW MY LIFE CHANGES ...

Since writing that first paragraph I became so busy that I didn't have time to write any more. However, now it is 1 July 2011 and I have decided that I must make time to write this book.

Remembrance Day this year will mark the ruby anniversary of my guide dog journey, and I want to write a tribute to my six dogs, all of whom have given me companionship and the confidence and independence needed to carry out my voluntary work, keeping me safe and preventing me from having any accidents.

In those early days with Topsy I never dreamt that a dog could do all the things that my six dogs have done. Although I did write a little about each dog in Just Jill, I will go into quite a lot of detail in this book so that people with no experience of blindness or guide dogs will be able to understand a little of the life of a blind person and the fantastic work that guide dogs do. Generally, most people that meet me want to know the name of my dog, how long I've had her and how old she is, which takes a bit of thinking about, especially if I'm queuing up to buy a railway ticket and my mind is on the job in hand. I suppose it keeps my brain working well.

Since my last book was published, I was awarded an OBE in the 2011 New Year's Honours, 28 years after receiving an MBE. Back in 1983 my third guide dog, Brandy, wasn't allowed to accompany me to the award ceremony, but you'll have to wait for Amanda's story to find out what happened on this occasion.

One hundred people go blind every day in this country, and I sincerely hope that this book will help them to cope with their new way of living and encourage them to consider having a guide dog if they're fit enough to do so.

FOREWORD

This fascinating book takes us behind the scenes of the partnership between a blind person and her guide dog and gives a highly readable and moving account of what that partnership really means.

Jill Allen-King is already known to many as a tireless and inspirational campaigner for the rights of blind and partially sighted people. Her book Just Jill, published in 2010, gave a remarkable insight into her life, from losing her sight totally at the age of 24, on her wedding day through her struggle to regain her confidence and independence, to her continuing high profile and high octane work, now in her 70s, on behalf of blind and other disabled people.

This latest book tells the story of the six guide dogs who have supported Jill over the past 40 years and without whom her own story would be very different. As Jill tells us, no one who is sighted can really understand the relationship between a blind person and their guide dog. Each of Jill's guide dogs has shared important stages in her life and each, in their very different ways, has been an integral part of all that she has achieved. I have been privileged to know Jill and all of her guide dogs, and to work with her on transport and mobility issues over many years.

Behind the calm, confident image of a blind person and guide dog walking along the street with which we are all familiar is a demanding and at times stressful process for the blind person of learning to put their trust in the dog. For the dog too there is a steep learning curve and many obstacles and challenges along the way.

As Jill describes so vividly, not all partnerships work out and dogs – like people – have their own characteristics and personalities. The book starts with the loyal and devoted Topsy who gave Jill the confidence to travel again after losing her sight and with whom she started her lifelong campaigning work. But then, for a brief period, came Bunty whose over-exuberance and greed made life very stressful for Jill.

The death of a guide dog is particularly traumatic for a blind person and Jill writes movingly of the loss of her closest and most constant companions and the struggle to come to terms with starting again on the long process of training, familiarisation and confidence building with a new dog.

Through the story of working with her guide dogs Jill also charts a fascinating social history in which her own campaigning has played such a key part. She takes us from the early days of commonplace prejudice which banned guide dogs from local libraries and many other public places through to the opening up of opportunities to take guide dogs on overseas travel and – a particular triumph for Jill – to Buckingham Palace for her OBE investiture in 2011.

Jill's Leading Ladies is an intensely personal story of the part that her "best friends" have played in giving her back the freedom she had lost when she went blind. It is also a powerful chronicle of the obstacles of prejudice, ignorance and tradition that Jill has taken on and demolished – and that she still challenges today.

Best wishes

Ann Frye OBE

CHAPTER 1
THE EARLY YEARS

It was 1940. My dad was already serving as a soldier in the Second World War and my mum was living in Philmead Road, Benfleet, in Essex, in the bungalow my parents had bought in 1937 after their marriage in Enfield, Middlesex.

I was due to be born on 1 March, St David's Day, and my mum was hoping for a boy and had planned to call him David. Unfortunately, I was ten days late and I wasn't a boy, much to my mum's disappointment. I was named Jill Griffith.

As my dad was away, my mum was persuaded to go and stay with his parents in Enfield, my mum's parents having died early in her life. She didn't really want to make this move, and it was while in Enfield that all my problems started.

My mum took me to the clinic and I picked up the measles there. As a result, on my first birthday I was rushed to Chase Farm Hospital and then on to Moorfields Eye Hospital, where I had to have my left eye removed. The vision in my right eye wasn't perfect, so this did restrict my ability to read small print and see long distances.

I was very lucky to be able to go to an ordinary school, as really I should've gone to a special school for blind children. Although I was not allowed to go to Benfleet School, I was accepted at St Margaret's School, a small Church of England establishment at Bowers Gifford, which was two bus rides away. I was able to take part in all the school's activities. In 1951 I transferred to King John's at Hadleigh, where again I participated in all activities, including netball and hockey, although I struggled with small print and had to sit at the front of the class to see the blackboard.

At the age of 15 I left school and did a two-year City & Guilds course in Hotel and Catering at Southend Municipal College, which included weekend work experience in hotels and restaurants in Southend.

On leaving college, my first full-time job was for the Shell Petroleum Company in London, working five days a week and catering for 2,000 people. I worked there for five years, until the company moved their premises to the South Bank, which would've made the journey too long for me. As it was, I used to catch the 6.25 train every morning and didn't get home until 6 p.m.

In the evenings I would go dancing three nights a week and attend the Girls' Life Brigade once a week.

In 1962 I started work as a directors' cook at Gallaher's in Cannon Street, London, and stayed there until June 1964, when I got married.

I'd met my husband at the Studio Dance Room at Chalkwell in Westcliff five years earlier and we'd saved up to buy our house, which was located just around the corner from the Studio. I still live there today.

So I was living a very active life, taking my gold medal for ballroom and Latin American dancing, running a Girls' Life Brigade company at Hadleigh and working full-time as a cook in the City of London.

But then my life changed forever ...

CHAPTER 2
ADJUSTING TO A WHOLE NEW LIFE

It was 6 June 1964. I was 24 years old, very fit and happy and leading a very busy, active life.

As planned, my wedding to Mick Allen took place at my church, followed by a wedding reception at the Westcliff Hotel. What wasn't planned was that I would go blind that day, too.

During my wedding reception my one and only good eye started to go blurry. Then finally, as I was cutting my wedding cake, my vision went completely, accompanied by quite a lot of pain. Despite this, we headed off to Eastbourne for our honeymoon, expecting that my eye would improve. No such luck. The following day I was admitted to Eastbourne Hospital.

After three weeks in Southend Hospital, where I'd been transferred as it was closer to home, and following an unsuccessful operation, I went to stay with my mum for three weeks, before eventually moving into our new home: a three-bedroom terraced house in Silversea Drive, Westcliff.

So there I was, newly married, totally blind, and unable to go back to my job as a cook in London, run my Girls' Brigade company or carry on dancing.

I had to adjust to a whole new way of living.

Mick went to work every day as an electrician, so most of the day I was on my own and, in the absence of any contact from Social Services, I had to teach myself how to cope.

It was the simple things of life that a sighted person takes for granted that I found difficult. After cleaning my teeth with my husband's hair cream because the tubes were the same shape and size, I quickly learnt that I had a nose and had to use it. No longer could I look in the mirror to brush and comb my hair. I still think one of the most depressing things of all is picking up the post and not being able to read it all, especially on birthdays and special anniversaries.

Money was the biggest worry of all. We'd bought our house on a joint 20-year mortgage and I didn't know how we were going to manage now that I was no longer able to work. Fortunately, my dad was able to arrange for our mortgage to be extended to 40 years, which reduced the monthly payments, but we still couldn't afford to buy items such an electric toaster, fridge or washing machine, which would've made my life a lot easier. We really were poor.

The good news was that I found out I was pregnant, but not everyone was so pleased. The doctors at Southend Hospital thought I should have an abortion. Although I won the battle to have my daughter, I was persuaded to have a sterilisation. This is something I've regretted all my life. It was put to me that if I had any more children my eye wouldn't get better, and at that time getting my sight back was more important than having another child. However, when I visited Moorfields a couple of years later a doctor told me that my vision couldn't be improved as the optic nerve had been destroyed by the measles. So the attitude of the doctors at Southend and Rochford hospitals, it would seem, was that a blind person shouldn't bring up a child.

Fortunately Gallaher's, where I'd worked as directors' cook for two years, paid me for a year, right up until my daughter Jacqueline was born. Without this money we would've lost our house.

Having Jacqueline was a blessing and it gave me something to live for. I wanted to bring her up just as well as if I'd been sighted, but it wasn't easy. Fortunately, however, Mick only worked a short bike ride away, so he was able to come home every lunchtime to help me.

It wasn't until Jacqueline was six weeks old that my GP, Dr Pearson, arranged for me to have a home help, as the hospital had made no provision for this. Also, it was several months before a social worker for the blind came to visit me, and that was only after Mick had seen a local charity collecting for the blind at the top of our road. They were collecting for a Christmas dinner and a summer coach trip to Felixstowe, neither of which were of much help to me as a housebound young mother with a baby. I had no one to take me out except for my husband at weekends and after my dad left work.

The social worker offered me a talking book player from the RNIB, which arrived 18 months later, and a white stick, but without any training in how to use it. This would be the focus of my first campaign a couple of years later.

CHAPTER 3
MY FIRST CAMPAIGN

Jacqueline was three years old, and up until that time I'd never been out on my own. One day, however, I decided that I would take Jacqueline for a walk around the block. I knew that eventually I was going to have to take her to school, and I had no idea how I was going to do that.

I'd started listening to Radio 4's *In Touch* programme, which offered useful information for blind people, and one day they talked about a long-cane training course due to be run in Birmingham. It would've been impossible for me to take part, however, as it was a six-month course and I couldn't leave Jacqueline for that length of time. I wrote to Southend Council to ask them if they could send someone on the course to be trained as a mobility officer, so that he could come back and train not only me but also the other 600 blind people living in Southend at that time.

Eventually, after writing several letters to the council and talking to local councillors, a Mr Denny was trained as a mobility officer, and he started to teach me how to get around using the long white cane. Training began in my home and focused initially on the correct way for Mick to guide me, i.e. by standing on the opposite side to the cane. A blind person wouldn't normally use a cane or stick indoors, but this was a good way to boost the confidence of a newly blind person.

I learnt that doors should be left either shut completely or wide open, and I was taught to walk while holding my arm across my body at an angle, with the back of my hand facing outwards, so that I could feel any obstacle in front of me.

From training in our house we moved to our church, where I learnt to walk first with Mick guiding me and then with the long cane. The church had long corridors and flights of stairs of different lengths, including a spiral staircase. Then, after a couple of weeks, my training moved to the street, and just by walking down my street I found all the obstacles that had stopped me from going out for the past five years. These obstacles are still present on most of the UK's residential streets and can be alarming for a blind person as well as being potentially dangerous.

For instance, suddenly encountering overhanging branches, trees and bushes can be a frightening experience at the best of times, but if they're prickly they can really hurt you. Residents shouldn't let them overhang the footpath, and councils can charge people for cutting them back if no action is taken following a warning.

Also, children will often leave their toys lying on the pavement when they've finished playing with them, which can be a real hazard for a blind person. Obviously I don't want to stop children from playing out, but if only they could be taught to put their toys back in their gardens or homes when they've finished with them. This applies to bicycles, too.

I think that children riding bikes or scooters should be trained to stop if they see a person using a stick, whatever colour it might be, as it can really shake your confidence when a bicycle flies past you and you don't know what's happening. Despite the fact that it is illegal to ride a bike on the pavement, many adults still do this and larger, faster bikes cause even more alarm.

At one time all bikes had to have a bell, but this requirement was removed in the 1970s at the request of the Pedestrians

Association, as bells were considered a nuisance. However, after years of campaigning on this issue, all new bikes must be equipped with a bell, although there is no requirement to use it. At least a bell gives some warning of an approaching vehicle.

Moreover, cyclists don't have to be trained before they're allowed to ride a bike and they don't have to be insured or own a licence, as with a car. So if a bicycle knocks you down and injures you or, worse still, causes a fatality, it would be very difficult to claim compensation from the rider.

Another obstacle that has to be negotiated is rubbish bags or wheelie bins, despite the fact that councils ask residents not to leave them on footpaths. I've actually known these bags to block the pavement completely. Even street furniture such as lamp posts, post boxes, seats, litter bins and bollards present a hazard for blind people.

Utility companies are also guilty of blocking pavements while carrying out work, and quite often the necessary safety measures are not put in place. A one-metre-high solid barrier is the only safe way to prevent someone from walking into an unguarded hole and other works, and at night they should be well lit.

In addition, there are sometimes cars and lorries parked on the pavement. Not only do these present another hazard in themselves, but also they can damage the pavement. Thousands of accidents every year happen to people that trip and fall on these cracked and broken surfaces.

So I was trained to walk around my local streets and to the local church, where Jacqueline would be attending nursery school, and also to Chalkwell School where she would go when she was five years old, but unfortunately I didn't receive any training on using a bus or a train. So, although I was able to take

Jacqueline out, I didn't have enough confidence to use the cane to go to the shops or venture further afield on my own.

It was a big day when Jacqueline was set to attend nursery school at the church hall for the first time. The social worker for the blind had arranged to meet me there and walk back with me, but she never turned up. So that was my first walk on my own. Fortunately, there was just one road to cross and it only took me about five minutes, but at the time I felt very let down and upset.

Jacqueline went there for about a year, until she started at the big school when she was five.

CHAPTER 4
SOWING THE SEED

Since going blind seven years earlier, I had been both encouraged and discouraged in terms of having a guide dog.

My first social worker never mentioned a guide dog, and the second one told me that they left a lot of mess and were unable to enter so many places that it would probably be best for me to stick with a white cane, although she took no steps to get me trained. The third social worker, who visited me a couple of times, was blind. His sighted wife used to accompany him in order to guide him and he was driven to his appointments by a council worker. He told me that a guide dog would hinder me from getting a job, as many employers would not allow dogs on their premises.

These were the people that I had expected to encourage me to train with a guide dog. Remember, I was only in my twenties, I was fit and healthy, and I had a young child to take out.

I started going to a young wives group at my church, and one evening they showed a film produced by The Guide Dogs for the Blind Association (GDBA) called *Leading Lady*. This planted a seed in my head about one day owning a guide dog, but the process described would involve a four-week course at Leamington Spa Training Centre and at that time I couldn't leave Jacqueline for such a long period.

The young wives attended an area meeting and it was there that I met Betty, who was accompanied by her guide dog, Jack, a large black Labrador. This was the first guide dog I'd ever met.

Betty said she would visit me one afternoon and I couldn't

understand how she would be able to find my house, which was a 25-minute walk from her home. When she arrived she explained that her husband had gone through the route with her, explaining the roads she would have to cross and telling her that my gate was the second one from the corner. We'd put raised numbers on the gate to make it easier for blind visitors to find the right house.

I was so impressed when she arrived and simply couldn't believe that a dog could take her on such a long and complicated journey and locate my house.

We sat in the garden and chatted, and I discovered that tape measures were available in Braille, at a cost of only two shillings, as well as knitting patterns. The social workers knew I could knit but had never mentioned these simple but incredibly useful aids. This information would have encouraged me to learn Braille.

Betty told me all about the work of guide dogs and it certainly sparked my interest. She, too, said that there were many places that guide dogs were not permitted to enter. She'd been refused access into the restaurant of a large store called Keddies, located in Southend high street.

Until I saw that film and talked to Betty I knew nothing about guide dogs. There had never been a talk at my school on the subjects of blindness or guide dogs. So I have spent the last 40 years doing just that.

By the time Jacqueline was three years old I'd started entering her in the Southend Carnival fancy dress competitions. We took one of the costumes, 'Jack in Her Box', with us when we went to Butlin's holiday camp at Bognor Regis in Sussex, and she was awarded first prize. We also came first in the mother and daughter competition, for which we wore matching dresses and had our hair done in the same style. While we were there we met a blind man called Tony. He, like me, was there with his young family. He'd just been trained with his first guide dog, but sadly the holiday camp wouldn't permit guide dogs.

Jacqueline was four years old when I started taking a Girls' Brigade company again, this time at Hadleigh Congregational Church. One of the girls suggested collecting silver paper to raise money for a guide dog for me, as the children's television programme *Blue Peter* was running the same scheme. So that's what we did over the next ten years.

Another blind man I'd met, who lived near Mick's work, came to see me and took me for a walk round the block one day. He said he didn't need a guide dog as his wife and three children could take him out. He worked in London and travelled there every day by train, so he'd got used to that regular routine. I didn't want Jacqueline to grow up thinking that she was responsible for taking me out. I wanted to be independent and felt that one day I would have a guide dog. But there were still too many buts, and I needed to feel that I really wanted a guide dog without any buts.

My final decision was made on my 31st birthday. My dad had phoned me from work, as he did every day, and had asked if my mum had been to see me. I told him she hadn't. Then I found out the following day that she'd been to the theatre not far from my house, but she hadn't called round or phoned me. This really upset me. My mother hadn't wanted to take me out very much after I went totally blind. It was her way of dealing with the fact that she hadn't taken me to the doctor quickly enough when I was a baby, resulting in me losing my left eye.

This spurred me to write off for a guide dog application pack. The forms were filled in and sent off, so now I just had to wait until the day arrived for me to be trained with my first guide dog.

CHAPTER 5
GUIDE DOG TRAINING, 1971

I was accepted for training after having a medical with my own doctor. Jacqueline was now six years old, and it was arranged that my neighbour, Mrs Marlow, would take her to school each morning. Mick would get her up, washed and dressed and give her breakfast, and then he would take her across the road to Mrs Marlow's when he left for work. Mick was quite capable of cooking an evening meal. Mind you, I think it was chips and beans most nights, plus the meat of the day.

On the Sunday before I went, I was sitting in church when a person behind me said, "You know, you won't be allowed in our shop." This was Dixons, another large store in Southend high street. The number of places that I'd been told guide dogs weren't allowed could quite easily have stopped me from getting a guide dog, and at that time I didn't know how I was going to handle the problem. However, I very quickly learnt once I arrived home with Topsy.

Mick took a day off from work to drive me the 200 miles to Leamington Spa in Warwickshire for my four-week training course. It was Friday 15 October 1971 and I had been blind for seven years. I hated leaving Jacqueline and Mick, but I knew it was going to be the best for all of us.

At that time Leamington Spa was the nearest training centre. It was named Edmond Scot Manor and was owned by The Guide Dogs for the Blind Association (GDBA), a charity funded by the public with no help from the Government.

On arrival I was met by my trainer, Lee Mitchell. He was young and had an even younger assistant, Neil Ewitt, who later became head of the puppy-breeding centre at Bishop's Tachbrook close by. I was taken to a single room, which would be my home for the next four weeks.

After Mick had left I met up in the large lounge with the other 11 students that would be trained with me. My initial observation was that some of them weren't totally blind like me. This was the first time I'd mixed with a group of blind people, and I found out that you could be registered blind even though you still had some vision. One man even had a newspaper delivered each day, and another would tell us when the trainer was walking past the window. I was also surprised to learn that some of the students had lost their vision due to measles, just like me.

We were all treated equally, whatever level of vision we had. A couple of the students had to wear a blindfold to start with. Blindfolds were also used as part of the trainers' training, which I thought was a good idea.

We spent Friday just learning our way around the large building and grounds. Then on Saturday we went for a long walk around the local streets, followed by a walk into town on the Sunday morning.

After lunch we all sat in the lounge, where we were given the equipment for our dogs: a harness, a brush and comb, a shammy leather, a bell collar, a short white stick, and an arm band to wear for safety. We were then each told the name of our dog, plus the colour and breed. I was to have Topsy, a black Labrador.

We then all went to our rooms and waited patiently until our trainers brought us our dogs. I was left with Topsy for about ten minutes so that I could get to know her. We were all then taken down to the lounge, where our dogs had to sit under our chairs, still on their leads. This was good training for when we were out and about in public places.

I can still remember those basic training sessions, which I think are missed now that those training centres no longer exist. We had lessons in grooming, feeding and obedience as well as lectures in a range of subjects designed to enhance our understanding of our dogs.

Topsy was 22 months old and had been puppy walked by Mr Phillipson, Director of Training. She, together with her sister, had been donated to the GDBA by a farm in Cambridge and had spent six months with Mr and Mrs Rodgers, who lived in Enfield, Middlesex, being trained as a guide dog puppy. It was a strange coincidence, as my grandparents had lived in Enfield, too, and I'd been staying with them when I caught the measles and lost my left eye as a child. The Rodgers also had a daughter of the same age as Jacqueline who was in the Girls' Life Brigade, so Topsy had been used to going to church. Even more strangely, my grandfather said he'd always wanted a little black girl called Topsy, and in fact he'd bought my grandma a doll called Topsy, which I still have.

I couldn't wait to phone home to tell Mick and Jacqueline about Topsy.

Then on the Monday morning the real work started.

Topsy had a bed in my bedroom, and it was lovely on the first morning when she came and woke me with a kiss. That was the signal that she wanted to go out to the toilet. We had been allocated a run for our dogs for this purpose and kennel girls and boys would come and clean the runs from time to time.

Dogs undergoing training were housed in a very large set of kennels and It was only when they were in their final month of training that they were allowed into the house. The kennel staff looked after these dogs and gave them their free runs, food and grooming.

To begin with we would leave our dogs in our rooms while we went for breakfast. This was a very social time. Each student would sit next to a member of staff, ranging from kennel girls to the manager of the centre, and each mealtime you would sit next to someone different. Therefore, over the four weeks of training you would get to meet all the staff.

At 9 a.m. half the class would go out in the minibus to a quiet area for outdoor training, while the rest of the class would undergo training in obedience and grooming. Then we would all meet up for coffee before each group swapped programmes.

In the grounds there was an obstacle course, which was really good for training us to walk through narrow spaces.

Initially my trainer would have a lead clipped onto Topsy's collar in order to supervise me closely. One day I was walking along a long pavement, working Topsy, when all of a sudden I stopped at a kerb. In front of me was a car. My trainer leaned out of the car and said to me, "Well done. You've been walking on your own for five minutes." He'd unclipped his lead without my realising it, walked off and got into a car further down the route to monitor my progress from a distance before rejoining me.

It was a most wonderful feeling to think I'd been led by Topsy. It gave me back all the confidence I'd lost when I went blind.

I noticed that Topsy was weaving as she walked and so I said to the trainer, "Why is she doing that?"

Lee replied, "She's guiding you round the fallen conkers."

She was also guiding me around the overhanging branches. That Topsy could give this kind of help was quite amazing. These overhanging branches, as mentioned earlier, are a real hazard to blind and partially sighted people, and can also prove to be a dangerous obstacle for sighted people on dark nights where the streets aren't well lit. Sometimes these trees and bushes hang over so much that they block the pavement and the dog has to take you out into the road to get around them. It would be so helpful if residents could cut them back.

We also encountered many cars parked on the pavement and, once again, Topsy had to take me out into the busy road to get around them. I was taught the correct and safe way to do this.

In all these situations, as well as when helping you to cross a road, a guide dog will stop and sit at the kerb. When the blind person thinks it is clear, they will give the instruction, "Forward", but the dog will only obey if it is indeed clear. If unsure, then it's best to wait for a sighted person to offer assistance. If you ever do offer to help a blind person cross the road, you should always approach them on the opposite side to their mobility aid and say, "Would you like any help?" If assistance is needed, the blind person will take your arm and you should escort them right across the road. If you know the blind person's name, then use it, and also give them your name. If you're a police officer, then explain who you are, as a blind person cannot see your uniform.

I was trained how to negotiate zebra crossings and ordinary sets of traffic lights. I'd been taught how to do this with a long cane, but it was so much easier with a guide dog. Traffic seemed to notice you more and stop when you had a dog rather than just a white cane.

I learnt to ignore drivers that honked their horns, as there was no guarantee that the hoot was meant for me or was an indication that it was safe to cross. The best help a driver can give is to get out of their car and escort the blind person across the road in the manner explained above.

I had to undergo two weeks of training before Mick and

Jacqueline were allowed to visit me and meet Topsy. Sunday afternoons were the only time we had off during our four weeks of training, and on the day they were due to arrive we went out for a long Sunday morning walk to Warwick and back, which was six miles in total. Mick actually saw me as he passed by in his car en route to the training centre. He commented afterwards that Topsy and I both had the same wobble. Well, they do try to match the dog with the person!

In the final two weeks we were trained to travel by bus and train, taking short journeys first of all with our trainers before going out on our own. One day we were dropped off on a large housing estate and had to find our own way back to the minibus. On a couple of occasions we also went to a small cafe in Leamington Spa's high street, to train the dogs to sit under the tables and be well behaved in that environment. They had been trained not to receive titbits, so it was important that they didn't look for food in eating establishments or food shops.

In the evenings we had lectures on a wide range of topics, one of them being about feeding. We were told the quantity of food to give the dog each day and not to give any extra titbits, in order to keep them healthy and fit.

These evenings were very helpful, especially to those of us that were new guide dog owners. Some on the course had owned a guide dog before, and they were able to help the first-timers. I certainly learnt a lot and made many new friends.

Towards the end of the fourth week the manager of the centre took each dog/owner pairing out and about to assess whether they would pass as a guide dog unit. So we were both put to the test, to ensure both that Topsy was good enough to be a guide dog and that I was good enough to work with her as a unit.

It was on 11 November 1971 that Topsy and I were called to the manager's office, so that the papers could be signed and I could be deemed officially qualified. It was a wonderful moment.

Mick and Jacqueline came up the following day to take Topsy and me home. As I knew that my daughter would want to make a fuss of Topsy, I asked my trainer, Lee Mitchell, to talk to Jacqueline about the way she should treat her. He told her that when Topsy was in her bed she shouldn't talk to her or touch her, as that was her space and her time to rest and be quiet. Also she was told not to talk to Topsy when she was working, which is advice I give to everyone. You should always ask the blind person first before touching or talking to a guide dog.

It was lovely to come home with Topsy on that Friday evening and start my new life. She was going to change me from a housebound person with no confidence into an independent person with the confidence to face a life of campaigning.

CHAPTER 6
TOPSY

1971

On the Saturday morning Mick left for work and I decided I would take Jacqueline to the library to change her books, a task that up until now Mick had always done. Topsy needed to learn her way around my home area, as it was all new to her, so we left home and made the ten-minute walk to Westcliff library. I was really thrilled to think I could take Jacqueline all by myself with Topsy guiding me.

We went into the library, handed in the old books and then went to the children's section to select some new ones. After a few minutes a lady came up to me and said, "Would you mind waiting outside with your dog. I will look after your daughter." Well, I was shocked, and Jacqueline was very upset. I'd already been warned that there were many places that wouldn't allow guide dogs, but I didn't expect the library to deny us entry. I refused to go outside and leave Jacqueline inside, so we went home without any books.

This incident at the library made me determined to campaign to improve access for guide dogs.

When we got home I phoned a friend I'd met in hospital to tell her what had happened, as I was very upset. My friend Barbara told me that her father-in-law worked for the council and would sort it out for me, which he did. However, when Mick went to the library on the Monday to get Jacqueline's books and spoke to the staff about the Saturday episode the response was, "Oh yes, we've got to let her in now." I never did go back to the library.

I'd just joined the National Federation of the Blind (NFB), so I had the opportunity to campaign on this access issue. Before I went to my first Federation meeting I was asked to attend a meeting at Southend Civic Centre, where an access committee was being formed. This would be the first access committee in the country. The committee comprised local people with different kinds of disabilities and members of council staff, and it was chaired by a councillor, Mrs Bullock Jarman. Meetings were held on a monthly basis and I attended them regularly over a period of ten years.

It opened my eyes about the needs of those with other disabilities, and I certainly learnt that the local council regarded us as a minority group and really neither wanted to listen to our concerns nor understood our problems. Everything we wanted we had to fight hard for.

Access to the local swimming pool was the first item on our agenda and was so for years, followed by the need for toilets that could be used by people in wheelchairs. I also started to tackle the guide dog issue, which eventually resulted in all the restaurants and shops accepting guide dogs.

Every day I would take Jacqueline to school, and after dropping her off I would go into Chalkwell park and meet some other mothers with their dogs. I would let Topsy off the lead so that she could have a free run with the other dogs. She had a bell on her collar so that I could hear where she was, and I also had a whistle to call her back. Two of the ladies there, Rene Rodgers and Jean Stewart, would escort me on a long walk around the park while the dogs were playing.

Apart from taking Jacqueline to school, I was thrilled to think that I could go out now whenever I wanted rather than rely on someone else to take me out. Doing my own shopping was the best thing of all. At that time we had a butcher, greengrocer, chemist, post office and newsagent, so Topsy had to learn each shop by name, which she did quite quickly.

A home help, paid for by the council, still came each morning to help me with my housework. At that time this service was available for any blind person who needed it. My home help was called Pat and she was with me from when Jacqueline was 18 months old up until she was 12. At that point the council started charging for the service and we just couldn't afford it anymore.

After lunch each day I would take Topsy out for a long walk and would normally go and visit a friend. We quickly learnt different routes. I had to take Topsy for six-monthly check-ups at the vet's, so this became one of my regular journeys. It was 12 turnings away, so to help me remember the roads I'd crossed I would put 12 coins in one of my pockets, and every time I crossed a road I would transfer a coin to my other pocket. This was especially useful if someone stopped to talk to me and I lost track of where I was.

I started taking a Girls' Brigade company again, so Topsy would come to all the meetings and church parades.

The first Federation meeting I attended was in Gidea Park, about a half an hour's drive away. It was called the Essex and Metropolitan branch. After three years we formed our own branch in Southend, and that was when all the campaigning work started for real.

1972

I had started giving talks before getting Topsy. Jacqueline had started Sunday School when she was three years old and a friend at my church, Jill Welsh, had asked me if I would do a talk for the children in her Sunday School class. She wanted me to speak about how as an unsighted person I used my hands.

I'd just started to learn Braille, so I showed them some Braille and explained that when you can't read with your eyes you have to read with your fingers. I then showed them a face I'd made for my Girls' Brigade members, using material and all kinds of fasteners. The eyes were buttons and the eyelids buttonholes, the mouth was a zip, the nose was press studs, the ears were hooks and eyes, and the hair was plaited wool. I'd also knitted a poodle, which I'd started making while I was in hospital having Jacqueline.

I had a draughts board designed for blind children, and used to play with Jacqueline. The white squares were sunken, so that I could feel where the holes were to slot in the draughts, and the black counters were small and the white ones large.

Jill was also a schoolteacher, so once I'd got Topsy she started to recommend me to her friends and contacts in schools and churches.

The first school talk, which I recorded, was on 20 January 1972 at Southend High School, and my first church talk was on 8 February at Rochford Methodist Church. Throughout the year I gave 28 a total of talks, many involving raising money for guide dogs. A particularly special talk was when I was invited to be a guest speaker for the diamond jubilee of the Girls' Life Brigade in Derby on 21 May. By coincidence one of my neighbours, Alison, was one of the girls and she can still remember my talk.

Topsy was now two years old and she'd learnt to sleep through my presentation and then wake up when the clapping started, thinking that the applause was for her. Whatever I spoke about, the questions always centred on Topsy.

During most of the summer months I would be creating the carnival float for Southend Carnival, which took place in August.

I would spend hours making crêpe paper flowers, which Mick would stick onto the model float he'd made.

It generally takes about six months to get used to working with a guide dog and during that initial period Topsy had certainly learnt her way around Westcliff.

On Tuesdays and Fridays we would go to the butchers to get our meat and I used to take a small shopping trolley, which I had to pull behind me. I'd been told during my training that I shouldn't do this, as a guide dog is only trained to allow for the width of the blind person and not anything they might be carrying. Of course, blind people with young children have to pull prams and pushchairs, so exceptions do have to be made, and Topsy coped very well with my trolley.

On my first trip to a shop Mick would accompany us so that Topsy knew where the shop was located, and when I went to the butchers for the first time on my own Topsy found it without any problem. Once I'd entered a shop I would just say to Topsy, "Find the counter," and she would. She would then sit and wait while I was being served and then guide me out of the shop and back home.

This first year with Topsy was spent working locally and getting used to taking Jacqueline to school every day, going to church on Sundays and visiting friends and my parents at Benfleet.

The first real access problem nationally came when Jacqueline was taking part in the Girls' Brigade rally at the Royal Albert Hall in London. I contacted the Albert Hall to find out if I could take Topsy with me and I was told I couldn't. So for the first time I had to leave Topsy with my friend Peggy Gargan. Although it was nice to attend the rally, I was naturally depressed at not being able to see Jacqueline in the display and not having Topsy with me. I wrote many times to the Albert Hall before they changed their policy and allowed access for guide dogs.

In my talks I was able to tell people about the wonderful independence you can have with a guide dog, but also the discrimination you face in the community and the effect it can have on you and your family.

That first year ended with Topsy blotting her copybook. Mick had taken Jacqueline and me down to the Christmas Carol concert at our church. When he got back he found that Topsy, who'd only been left for ten minutes, had removed a parcel from beneath the Christmas tree. The present was a box of sweets that Jacqueline had saved up to buy for her dad. Out of all the parcels that were there, Topsy had to find that one! We quickly learnt not to leave such items at a low level again.

1973

I'd already become a member of the Executive Council of the National Federation of the Blind (NFB), which meant attending quarterly weekend meetings in London. Mick would take Topsy and me by car for these, but I would go by train for any other meetings in London.

A train journey to London meant a half-an-hour walk to Chalkwell railway station, as there was no bus service there even though we lived in a built-up area of Westcliff, and Topsy very quickly learnt this route. On arrival at the station she would find the booking office so that I could buy my ticket and then take me down two flights of steps to the platform. Topsy had very short legs and on three occasions she actually slipped between the edge of the platform and the train when trying to board it. Fortunately, she wasn't hurt, but it frightened me enough never to get on a train without help from a sighted person.

On disembarking at Fenchurch Street station I would instruct

Topsy to follow the other passengers. On one occasion I hadn't realised that we'd already reached and gone through the ticket barrier, at which point I would tell Topsy to find the stairs, so I was still telling her to follow the other people. As a result, she ended up following the men into the gents' toilet! I think the men were more shocked than me, as I said I could smell where I was!

Once through the ticket barrier Topsy would find her way down the stairs to the taxi rank. At that time we hadn't learnt to use the underground.

The NFB was founded in 1947 but it had never campaigned on access or transport issues, so in October an environment committee was formed. I was elected as its chairperson and that was when the real hard work started.

On of my first tasks was being part of a delegation that attended a meeting with the Guide Dogs for the Blind Association (GDBA) at its headquarters in Windsor. At that time the Guide Dog Council had no members that were guide dog owners and no representatives from organisations of blind people. Following the meeting it was agreed to set up a liaison committee, which would comprise two members from the NFB, two members from the Circle of Guide Dog Owners and the Chairman of the Council. Normally the director and the chief executive would also be present. This committee met every quarter for ten years, and I attended all these meetings, which was a very long journey for Topsy and me.

An item that was always on the agenda at these meetings was the question of access to public buildings, hotels, restaurants and transport. the GDBA was very reluctant at that time to get too involved in campaigns, so campaigning was really left up to me and the NFB.

I can remember at one of the first meetings telling them about the time we'd been visiting relatives near Brighton and had wanted to take Jacqueline onto the pier. However, on entering the pier we'd been told that guide dogs weren't allowed. I couldn't understand this, as we'd had no problems with Southend pier.

At that time the Central Council for Disabled People displayed a sign on any building that was accessible for people using wheelchairs, and I wanted them to include a guide dog symbol as well. After some correspondence it was decided that we would have our own sign, which said: 'NO DOGS ALLOWED EXCEPT GUIDE DOGS'. These signs are still used and are available from the GDBA.

Life was very busy with all these meetings and, in addition, this year I gave 57 talks to schools, churches and other groups. Many of these made a donation to the NFB, as we were going to start a new branch in Southend, and many schools were raising money for guide dog training.

We were still collecting silver paper, too. It didn't raise much money, but every little helps and we thought it might encourage people to make monetary donations to the charity or leave money in their wills for guide dogs.

Every year we had a visit from my guide dog trainer, just to make sure that Topsy and I were still working as a unit and to check that I was feeding her the right amount of food. Labradors can so easily put on weight, so I weigh her food every day.

Being so busy certainly kept Topsy and me fit.

1974

This was a very eventful, busy year. Locally and nationally the access work was starting to achieve success.

Locally, we formed the Southeast Essex branch of the NFB in

Westcliff and after a few weeks we had 50 members. We started a Braille class at the library and a monthly swimming session at Southend pool, and on the third Saturday of the month we held a Torch Trust meeting.

Nationally, after writing many letters, we were able to elicit a change in the environmental health regulations, making guide dogs exempt. This meant that we could go into many restaurants that had previously denied access.

In addition to 45 talks, I organised my first national conference for the NFB, which was held at the Civic Centre in Southend. Around 150 delegates from all over the UK attended the conference, many travelling by train and plane and many accompanied by their guide dogs, and they were accommodated at the airport hotel and a couple of smaller hotels in the town.

One of our NFB members, from the Liverpool branch, had produced a sticker that would give me many years of work. We all knew the hazard caused by cars parking on pavements, so this blind man called Ernie had produced a sticker that said: 'YOUR CAR IS PARKED ILLEGALLY ON THE PAVEMENT. YOU ARE A HAZARD TO BLIND PEOPLE'. We would stick these on any cars we found parked on the pavement. Eventually we started the 'Give Us Back Our Pavement' campaign.

It was during this year that I joined the Liberal Party, and I was elected to stand as a candidate in the 1975 elections. This was going to be a new way of life for Topsy. With help from friends acting as guides, we canvassed most of the roads in the ward. Topsy thought it was great fun going up to all the doors, but was quite disappointed when we didn't get to enter each house. Unfortunately, I wasn't successful, but I learnt a lot from the experience. I also learnt all the roads in the area, which subsequently has been of great help not only personally but also for helping people who get lost in the area.

Another 45 talks and a carnival float also kept Topsy and me occupied this year.

1975

Jacqueline left her junior school at Chalkwell and started attending Belfairs School in Leigh, which meant a bus ride for her. For me and Topsy it meant a whole day to ourselves.

I'd become a representative for the NFB on the RNIB's Executive Council and had started to serve on many committees, involving regular train journeys to Fenchurch Street station in London for Topsy and me, followed by a half-hour taxi ride to Great Portland Street, where the headquarters of the RNIB were located.

Topsy hadn't been trained to go to the toilet in the gutter and would only go on grass, so when I was at the RNIB all day I would have to take her for a ten-minute walk to Regent's Park. This meant crossing four very busy roads. At the park she would find me a seat, and then on went her bell-adorned collar and off she would go, but only for five minutes as we had to get back for the meeting. No extra time was ever given to those of us with guide dogs at lunchtime or during tea breaks. Topsy was only fed once a day, so her dinner would have to wait until we got home.

One of the first committees I was on was the consumer committee. The 20 blind members would discuss consumer matters and test new pieces of equipment, such as Braille watches, white sticks, kitchen timers, board games, tin openers and many other household items. At that time there was provision for blind people to examine the items sold in the shop on the ground floor of the RNIB building. After many requests, a table was set up in the shop to display these items and eventually it was converted into a resource centre.

As we commonly experienced problems hailing a taxi, we had a card made displaying the word 'TAXI', with one corner cut off to make it easy to identify which way up it should be. As this was so successful, we had another card made that said 'YOUR HELP WELCOMED'. This one had two corners cut off so that we could differentiate between the two cards. Eventually a similar card was made for bus stops, to indicate to the driver what bus number we required.

All these very simple aids helped to make travelling around London a little easier. But, no gadget could ever replace the help that can be gained from a sighted person. However, the general public are very reluctant to offer assistance, especially if you have a guide dog. I will always accept help when given, even if I don't really need it. Refusing that help could make that person reluctant to offer assistance in the future and the next blind person may really need it.

During this year we attended many local and national meetings.

1976

The NFB's environment committee had raised a wide range of pavement and transport issues and had written many letters to the Department of Transport. As I'd become the NFB's public relations officer we were getting good publicity, and in 1976 the access problem hit the spotlight.

Colin Low, at that time general secretary of the NFB, had been appointed to a committee chaired by Lord Snowdon. This committee was looking at all the access problems for disabled people and Colin had told me to send Lord Snowdon copies of all the letters I'd received from the various companies that were denying guide dogs access. These included Butlins and Pontins holiday camps, Mecca bingo halls, Odeon cinemas, the Albert Hall, British Rail dining and sleeping cars, the House of Commons public gallery and, the one that brought everything to a head, the Chelsea Flower Show.

Two NFB members from Leamington Spa were members of their local Horticultural Society and had booked tickets to attend the Chelsea Flower Show, but they were told that their guide dogs wouldn't be allowed in. On receiving this information, Lord Snowdon wrote a letter to the *Times* newspaper, which was published and gave my name as the campaign leader. As a result, I was contacted by Radio 4's *Today* programme, and in the February Topsy and I were picked up very early by a car and taken up to Broadcasting House, where we were interviewed about access problems. However, it was several more years before guide dogs were allowed to attend the Chelsea Flower Show.

It was 17 September when Tony Castleton passed me as an official speaker for the GDBA, although I'd been giving talks ever since I first got Topsy.

Then, on 28 October, Topsy and I had our first visit to Buckingham Palace. One of the girls from the First Southend Girls' Brigade Company had spent a year helping me with my reading as part of the Duke of Edinburgh Award scheme. I was so pleased when she invited me to go with her parents to the award ceremony at the Palace. When we arrived I was asked if I would like Topsy to be looked after or whether I wanted to keep her with me. She stayed with me, of course, and she was very good, as usual.

Another 36 talks were given in this year.

1977

1977 was the Queen's Silver Jubilee year, so we made a two-tier 10ft cake for Southend Carnival, for which I made 10,000 crêpe paper flowers. We won first prize in the Southend Carnival and also in Burnham and Rochford carnivals. This was the last year that we did a carnival float, as Jacqueline was now playing trumpet in the Girls' Brigade band. In fact, they were the national champions and were chosen to lead a youth parade up The Mall to celebrate the Jubilee.

It was while I was making the flowers for the float that I met Alvin, who ten years later would become my second husband. Alvin had just got his first guide dog, a yellow Labrador called Unity. Our two dogs first met outside the butcher's shop just a few minutes' walk away from our house. Alvin was living in the next road.

Alvin was training to be a piano tuner in London and, on discovering that I always took a taxi from Fenchurch Street station when I was attending RNIB meetings, he wanted to know why I didn't use the underground. I told him I didn't have enough confidence to do so. From then on, every time I went to London, Alvin would travel with me and teach Topsy and me how to transfer from the train to the underground at Barking. At that time there were very few announcements on the train, and these are so important for blind people as otherwise you have no idea where you are.

All I had to do when I got off the train was walk across the platform and wait for a district line underground train to arrive. Sometimes I would miss a train because I didn't realise there was a train already waiting. There wasn't always a member of staff around to help me. We would then make the 20-minute journey to Aldgate, where we would get off and wait for a

Metropolitan line train to take us to Great Portland Street. On arrival Topsy would lead me out of the station and take me on the five-minute walk to the RNIB's HQ. These roads were very busy and noisy, but Topsy coped very well and was always happy working.

This was a very busy year for my talks. In all I did 68, including teaching people who were training to be social workers for the blind.

1978

1978 was just as busy, and it was in this year that the NFB launched the 'Give Us Back Our Pavement' campaign, aimed at the Department of Transport, the Police and the general public and with the goal of stopping parking and cycling on pavements and reducing the number of obstacles. We produced a series of leaflets, stickers and posters for the campaign.

The NFB didn't have an office at this time, so I was sending out around 30 letters a day, assisted by a friend called Ann Gretton.

I was able to publicise the campaign on the BBC Radio's Jimmy Young and John Dunn shows. Many blind people joined the NFB as a result of this campaign.

We were also campaigning for a blindness allowance, as at this time blind people received no financial benefits. On 3 May I spent most of the day outside Downing Street holding a poster. I went straight from there to the Thames Television studios in Euston Road and was interviewed together with my MP, Paul Channon.

Topsy always liked to be in a television studio. As she was a black dog, I always had to wear bright colours so that she would stand out. She was always ready to sit up and look at the cameras.

In the November I was invited for the first time to open a Bazaar, in a hall at Hockley not too far from my home. This was the highlight of that year for me.

Once again, I was busy with talks and did 57 to schools and church groups. I made many presentations of photos of guide dogs to those groups that had raised money to pay for the training of a guide dog, or in some cases two or three dogs.

I attended my first Liberal Party conference this year at Llandudno, accompanied by my friend Barbara. One day we took Topsy to the beach as she'd been very good sitting in the conference for hours. Topsy loved the water, and once she'd got into the sea she decided she didn't want to come out again. Although she was normally very good on recall, on this occasion she preferred swimming in the sea than going back to the conference. It just goes to show that even guide dogs can have their fun.

1979

This was one of the saddest years in my life. My dad, who'd been ill for many years with heart trouble, spent many weeks in Southend Hospital following a stroke and eventually died on 27 June. Even though I was busy with my talks and the pavement campaign, I still found time to walk up to the hospital every day to visit him.

Topsy had taken me to there many times in 1972 to visit my grandma, who was in there for three months before she died. There was no direct bus service, and it was about a half-hour walk from my house. I visited her nearly every day until she died on 13 October.

On these visits I used to arrive just as my grandma was having her afternoon tea. She would sit in an armchair just in front of me, and I would have Topsy wedged between my legs under my chair. Although I had full control over Topsy, the same couldn't be said for my dear grandma! Without my knowing it, she would throw bits of bread and cake to Topsy. Unfortunately, this encouraged Topsy to start looking for titbits all the time, and one day when we were at Gilbert's bakery she helped herself to a cream cake! It took quite a long time to wean her off this titbit-seeking habit.

My dad had been bitten by a dog not long before I got Topsy, so to begin with he'd been very nervous about my having a dog. However, once he'd seen the sort of life that Topsy had helped me to lead, he became very fond of her.

While my dad was in hospital the pavement campaign had a big press launch, and BBC TV's Kate Adie came and did a walk round the block with me, which was shown on the 9 o'clock news.

Although I still fitted in 50 talks this year, Topsy, now nine years old, wasn't well. She had a blocked bowel, caused by a piece of marrowbone getting wedged in her gut. These bones are supposed to be good for a dog's teeth, but Topsy wasn't allowed another one after this. She also had to have a cataract removed from her eye, but she still carried on working.

GDBA representatives would visit Topsy every six months to make sure that she was working well and was fit and healthy. One thing about guide dogs: you can't force them to work. If they don't want to work, they won't.

1980
We did slow down a bit in 1980, doing only 33 talks, but the meetings continued apace both in London and at home.

Whenever Topsy took me to a shop she would just go in the

door and take me straight to the counter. One day, when there was a bread strike, I walked up the road as normal and round the corner to my baker's shop, which was the third shop from the corner. We went through the door as usual and up to the counter.

The lady serving asked, "How long have you had to wait, Jill?" Slightly puzzled, I replied, "Not at all."

Apparently, due to the bread strike, a long queue of people had developed outside the baker's shop, extending right around the corner. However, Topsy had simply bypassed everyone and taken me straight to the front! As no one said anything to me, I was totally unaware of the situation! Topsy would often do the same at the bus stop or the railway station.

Topsy celebrated her 10th birthday with a party for all her guide dog friends. In those days all dog food came in a tin, so I made a cake out of these tins of food and put biscuit bones on the top to represent candles. I think there were six dogs and they all lay on the floor, with our cat Sparky sitting in the middle. Fortunately, guide dogs are trained to be around cats without any trouble.

1981

This was the International Year of Disabled People, and the Queen held a garden party for 4,000 people with disabilities at Buckingham Palace to mark the occasion. The NFB was allocated ten tickets and I was lucky enough to receive one of them.

Just a couple of days before we were due to go, I received a letter inviting me to have tea in the tent with the Queen and other members of the royal family. As it was July, I bought myself a light dress and jacket in a fine green and white check, together with a white hat. As the dress was a little long, a length was cut off. The spare material was made into a bow for Topsy and a band to adorn my hat.

As I was going on my own, I wasn't sure how I was going to find my way to the tea tent. I knew that Derrick Carver, the director of the GDBA, was going, so I asked him to help me. He ended up staying with me for the whole two hours I was there, which was a good job, as otherwise I wouldn't have known to whom I was talking.

It was just one week before Lady Diana married Prince Charles. Diana sat on the grass and stroked Topsy while she talked with me for ten minutes. The Queen also spoke to me and asked me what I did. I told her that I was campaigning to improve access for guide dogs, as there were still so many places we were not allowed to go. There were 40 other guide dogs at the garden party and all were very well behaved.

The following day I gave a talk at Westborough School and was able to tell the children about our exciting day at the palace. Topsy still had the strong scent of Lady Diana's perfume in her fur. It was one of those talks I shall never forget.

In the same month the GDBA was celebrating its Golden Jubilee, and hundreds of guide dog owners were invited to a service at Westminster Abbey. We then walked along the streets to Buckingham Palace, where we had tea. Princess Alexandra, the Patron of the GDBA, was present throughout the day.

On the walk to the palace, out of the crowds came a voice calling me. It was Miss Coates, who had been the head of the maternity service at Rochford Hospital, where Jacqueline was born. While I was in that hospital I had knitted poodles, and Miss Coates called out, "Jill, I've still got your poodle."

Although Topsy was now 11 years old, she was still fit enough to do this walk and it was lovely that she was with me for these very important celebrations.

In April a book was published called *Images of Ourselves*, which contained life stories of different women with a variety of disabilities. I wrote a chapter from the perspective of a blind housewife and mother.

Essex Radio started on 19 September, and I was able to write a daily script to help disabled people. My mum would help me to write these down, and then once a week Topsy would take me by train to the studios in Southend. I did this for five years.

One of the 54 talks I did this year was to the Social Services department in Plymouth, Devon. I can remember on the return journey, while we were stopped at Newton Abbot station, someone stole my talking clock. I'd placed it on the table in front of me so that I could check the time and know when to get off at Teignmouth, as I was going to stay overnight with my Auntie Rose. That really taught me not to trust anyone, and from then on I've always been very careful while travelling on trains. We'd set off from home very early that morning and it had been a long and tiring day for both of us without having to experience this upset.

One of the problems on such a journey is finding somewhere for Topsy to go to the toilet, as there is no provision for this at railway stations. On that day Topsy had to go the whole Southend to Plymouth trip without a toilet break. The general public are always complaining about dog mess, and yet no councils or public transport operators make any provision for dogs.

1982

Topsy celebrated her 12th birthday on 14 January. She was still working, but she didn't have much longer to live.

On 31 March we visited Stambridge School, where we'd gone

regularly to give talks. However, this was to be last school talk that Topsy and I did together. The very last talk we did was at St Mary's Church in Benfleet, which was just at the bottom of the road where my mum was still living.

I already knew that Topsy wasn't going to live very long, as she'd collapsed in Southend one day. A taxi took us to the vet's and, after some tests, Mr Downs told me that she'd got cancer. He said she had between three and eighteen months left, but in reality she only lived a further week.

On that sad day we'd done a normal short walk to the park in the afternoon, but when we got there she just sat looking around and didn't want to move. Then after about 15 minutes she got up and we went home. She worked just the same as the first day I'd got her. After her dinner a little while later she went to lie in the hall. She never got up again.

I called the vet and, after talking with me for a very long while, we decided that it was better to put her to sleep. My usual vet, Mr Downs, was on holiday and so a Mr Hepworth came out to see me and he was so kind. As you can imagine, I was heartbroken.

Mick dug a large hole in the middle of our lawn, and that's where Topsy was laid to rest. She had worked so hard and had been my best friend for over ten years. She had given me back all the confidence I had lost when I went blind, and she had led me safely all over the country. She had helped me to gain access to many places and had been the perfect example of a well-trained guide dog. She had helped me to raise thousands of pounds, not only for guide dogs but also for other charities.

Topsy died on 26 April and, although still very upset, I started my talks again on 10 May, making one of my regular visits to speak to the staff at Southend Hospital.

As Topsy had died quite suddenly, I had to wait until 9 July before I could be retrained with another guide dog at Leamington Spa. Jacqueline was now 17 years old and at college, so I didn't have to worry about leaving her as I had done the first time when she was only six years old.

And Bunty, my next dog, was a different kettle of fish to Topsy.

CHAPTER 7
BUNTY, 1982

Although the training would take the same form as it had done when I was trained with Topsy, I knew it would be different with a new dog. What I didn't know was just how different it would be and the new way of life that Bunty would bring.

From the moment we met in my room I just knew that she was going to be hard work. Bunty was a much larger dog than Topsy and was a yellow Labrador; in fact, she was almost white. She was a very pretty dog, which would lead to some of the problems I experienced with her. I came to the conclusion that having a new dog was harder than having a baby.

The training was just the same, but I had a different trainer this time. Graham Poole, who had trained Bunty, knew that she was much larger than Topsy but thought that I would be able to cope with her.

Right from the start Bunty wasn't as well behaved as Topsy. She tried to pick up anything she could in my room, so I had to hide everything from her. As soon as I started to work her, she pulled me all the time. Topsy had never done this, so I found it quite difficult to handle. The trainers on my course all tried to help slow her down, but she was determined not to oblige.

In spite of these problems, we completed the four-week training course and returned home on 30 July.

Mick and Jacqueline had driven up to Leamington to collect us, and on arrival home the first disaster happened. Mick opened the front door, and as I walked in with Bunty on her lead she just flew out of my control. She ran up the stairs and straight into

Jacqueline's bedroom, where she began to demolish the soft toys lying on her bed. The first thing to go was a lovely model of, I think, a snake, which was a door stopper. Obviously Jacqueline was very upset and I was very cross with Bunty. That was the start of a very difficult six months.

Bunty never stopped pulling, and I gradually started to get backache and stomach pains from the constant strain. Despite that, she was a very loveable dog and indoors always wanted to be cuddled.

Another problem arose when I started to go out to the shops with her. People living in the area had got used to me out and about with Topsy, and when I stopped to speak to them Topsy would just sit still and listen quietly. Everyone wanted to talk to Bunty, and however many times I asked them not give her any attention they still did. As a result, Bunty got very excited and then didn't want to work. I tried to explain the importance of people not speaking to a guide dog when it was working, especially a new dog that was still learning to work in a new area. One lady I used to meet in the post office told me I was being unkind because I wouldn't let her touch or talk to Bunty. I tried to tell her that if Bunty was distracted she wouldn't work, and if that happened then she would have to go back to the training centre.

My first talk with Bunty was on 2 September, when I visited the Hockley Ladies' Club. She was very good sitting beside me during the talk, but I did have to keep tight control of her. The children at my school talks loved her, because she had a very pretty face, and they thought it was great fun that she'd been a bit naughty and taken Jacqueline's toys.

More problems cropped up due to her almost white hair. My red carpets, even though they were hoovered every day, always looked like a tartan pattern. In addition, I was doing a lot of travelling on the trains at that time, and London businessmen in dark suits didn't appreciate being covered in Bunty's hairs. Also, it was a very hot summer that year and Bunty liked to lick the feet of ladies wearing open sandals.

I had a very busy few months attending meetings all over the country with Bunty, and also every month the trainers came to see us to check on progress.

I spent quite a lot of time working with the Department of Transport, developing the tactile paving for pedestrian crossings. This idea began years earlier when Topsy used to take me every Thursday to visit a friend called Peggy in Highfields Grove. I knew when I'd reached her gate, as there was a run-in to a garage that I could feel under my feet. It was also flush with the road. Because kerbs were being flattened for wheelchairs and prams, blind people were risking serious injury due to not knowing if they were on the road or on the pavement. I suggested the compromise of a tactile surface in order to distinguish between them. After two years of research by the Transport and Road Research Laboratory, Bunty took me to test out this new texture. She also took me to Manchester, as there were plans for a cycle track to be built on the pavement and I needed to dissuade the authorities from pursuing this idea.

We made several trips on the Tilbury Ferry, travelling across to Kent to take part in broadcasts on Radio Medway, and we also opened two bazaars, one at Hockley and the other at Benfleet Methodist Church, the latter falling on Jacqueline's 18th birthday.

I had a few embarrassing moments with Bunty. On one occasion I was being filmed by Channel 4 television for a documentary about access for guide dogs. There was me, saying how well behaved guide dogs were, and at the same time there was Bunty, under the table chewing the cables! On another occasion Jacqueline was receiving a Student of the Year award at the Hotel and Catering college in Southend, which she'd been attending for the last two years. We were all sitting at long banqueting tables and Bunty was tethered securely, or so I thought, at my feet under the table. However, without anyone noticing, she'd struggled out of her chain collar and was found in the kitchen eating a tray of chicken!

The most frightening and most dangerous thing she did was chasing after another dog in Blenheim Park, running out of the gates and across a dual carriageway. This time she was found in the allotments eating vegetables. This was the last straw for me, as she could've caused a very serious accident.

Steve Wright, the manager of the training centre, came straight down to see me. By this time I'd had Bunty for around six months, and I was a physical and nervous wreck. Steve took me to Southend High Street, most of which was pedestrianised, and we walked from the bottom to the top. After that walk he said she'd picked up every chip lying on the ground and she would have to stop being a guide dog.

I was very upset and asked if there was anything I could do, so Steve said he would let me have a week's retraining at Leamington to see if I was doing anything wrong. It was the week before Christmas and I went out with every trainer each day. At the end of the week Steve apologised and said that they'd given me the wrong dog, and I know it's very difficult to match the right dog to the right person every time.

I came home with Bunty, feeling quite depressed and that I'd let her down. However, I then received a letter that cheered me up and helped me focus on the future. I was to be awarded an MBE in the New Year's Honours list. It was very difficult to keep this secret until 1 January. I didn't even tell my mum.

Although this year had been very sad with the death of Topsy and the troubles with Bunty, with their help I'd given 50 talks and raised a few thousand pounds for guide dogs.

CHAPTER 8
BRANDY

1983

I went back to Leamington Spa training centre with Bunty on 9 January. It was very sad giving her back, but I knew she wasn't the right dog for me. She was retrained and went out again as a guide dog, this time with a strong man.

So there I was, waiting in my room for my new dog. I had no idea what sort of dog it would be. Then the door opened and in came Brandy, a beautiful little golden Labrador. She was so much smaller than Bunty and had such a lovely silky coat. Mark Fisher, her trainer, knew all about my previous problems and assured me that Brandy was a very different kind of dog to Bunty.

On the day I left for Leamington I got a letter inviting me to Buckingham Palace on 10 February to receive my MBE. This meant that I had to complete my training in three weeks in order to be home in time to go to the Palace. One of the staff took me around the shops to buy a suit, which was really exciting. I chose an apricot-coloured dress and jacket that would match Brandy's coat.

The training was just the same as before, and it was lovely not being pulled. Working with Brandy was very much like working with Topsy. I came home on Sunday 6 February, feeling much happier with Brandy than I had with Bunty.

The next three days were spent getting ready to go to Buckingham Palace. Although I'd bought my suit in Leamington, I still had to buy my shoes, hat, bag and gloves. My Uncle

Bernard took me to some little shops in Leigh, where I bought all brown accessories.

Although I'd been to the Palace three times before with Topsy, I needed to check that I could take Brandy with me for the investiture. Lord Snowdon had been helping me with the access campaign, so I telephoned him and he assured me that everything would be all right.

The Department of Transport had arranged for a car to take me up to the Palace, and Mick and Jacqueline went with me. On arrival, we made our way to the designated door and were met by Palace staff. They told me they'd have to take Brandy off me, as she wasn't allowed to stay with me. This really upset me and I was very cross. The main reason for my getting an MBE was all the work I'd done to improve access for guide dogs, so it was ironic that Brandy was refused. Although I was escorted by Palace staff, I spent the whole time worrying about Brandy and this really spoilt my day.

After we'd left the Palace we were contacted by the press, and the following morning I was on the *Breakfast Time* programme on BBC television being interviewed by Selina Scott. Another guest was the Queen's dressmaker, Sir Norman Hartnell, who congratulated me on the clothes I was wearing. This really pleased me.

On returning home I was driven up to Norwich to take part in the evening programme, and also a statement was made in the House of Commons.

We started to do our talks again, but I didn't resume the meetings in London for about three months.

The first time we went to a meeting at the RNIB HQ, we were coming out of the lift when another dog went for Brandy. This really upset Brandy, and from that day on she was always nervous when she saw another dog and would forget about her work and try to have a go at it. I didn't have any accidents, but I did have a lot of near misses. It was a real shame, as she was such a lovely dog, and it just shows how one attack can cause lasting upset for a dog.

It was 18 July when the tactile paving was launched in Parliament Square by Tony Newton, MP, who was the Secretary of State for Social Security at the time. It was also the day that I left my husband Mick.

Brandy was such a comfort to me at this sad time in my life. Brandy and I stayed with Alvin in his flat a couple of roads away, until my divorce came through the following March.

We carried on going to meetings in London and giving talks locally, although we only did 23 this year.

One important event was when I was invited to the Cafe Royal in London for the Best of Britain awards, held on 11 December. My friend Barbara accompanied me and, just before I left, my friend Vivienne called in to give me a lovely orchid to wear.

Brandy was very well behaved, sitting under the table while we had our meal. Vera Lynn was the chief guest and it was wonderful to meet her, and Matthew Kelly was at our table.

This had been a very emotional year for me: losing Bunty, receiving an MBE and splitting up with my husband of 19 years. Without the love and affection of Brandy I couldn't have coped as well as I did.

1984

The year started with me still living with Alvin and his guide dog Remo, a golden retriever. Alvin was now working as a piano tuner, after finishing his four-year training course in London.

On 23 March my divorce became absolute, and Mick was still

living in our house with Jacqueline. Also on that date a new committee was established by the Government: the Access Committee for England. This committee was set up as a result of the work done by the Lord Snowdon committee. Colin Low, later to become Lord Low of Dalston, had been a member of that committee and had fed into it all the access problems I'd encountered, as well as other cases of discrimination.

I was appointed to be a member of the Access Committee for England, due to my experience as a member of the Southend Access Committee since its formation in 1971. Also, I had chaired the NFB's Environment Committee since its formation in 1973 and I was Chairperson of the Joint Committee on Mobility for Blind and Partially Sighted People.

At this time the Cycle Tracks Act was being debated in the House of Commons. I was already concerned about this issue, as people were riding their bikes on the pavements and causing lots of accidents to pedestrians. The new Act made provision for shared facilities, which meant that bikes would be allowed to share the same pavements as pedestrians. The Joint Committee was totally opposed to this, and I wanted to go and listen to the five-hour debate.

I arrived with Brandy at the entrance to the House of Commons public gallery, but I was refused entry and was taken back down to the lobby area while some questions were asked in the House. It made me very cross that I wasn't allowed in to hear that debate, as when you're campaigning it's important to hear other people's points of view. It wasn't until 1987, after 12 years of writing letters, that permission was given for guide dogs to be allowed into the public gallery.

One day, when Alvin and I were going to London, Alvin's guide dog got his tail caught in the train door. Fortunately, he didn't suffer any major injury, but he also had a lump on his leg that needed to be removed, which meant that he wouldn't be fit enough to guide Alvin on and off buses every day. As a result, he was retired and went to live with some friends as a pet until he died at the age of 17.

In the September, Alvin went back to Leamington Spa to be trained with his third guide dog, Francis.

On 7 December Mick moved out of our house, and on 20 December Alvin and I, with guide dogs Brandy and Francis, moved back in. My daughter Jacqueline, then 20 years old, lived with us until she moved into her own flat in 1988, and in 1990 she married Mike.

As I was attending so many more meetings in London, I only had time to do 20 talks this year.

1985

We were all settling into the house in Silversea Drive, and I'd been invited to speak at a National Bus conference in London.

I was scheduled to be the first speaker after the lunch break, and Brandy and I were sitting having our lunch when another guide dog had a snap at Brandy. I put my hand down to intervene and in the process my right hand got bitten by the other dog and I had to be rushed to hospital for treatment. Although I couldn't do my talk, I was well enough to go home. Brandy stayed with me all the time and, as usual, sat with her head on my knee going home. My hand and arm were bandaged for three weeks, so it was very difficult to work Brandy.

Alvin's mum came down and stayed for two weeks to help me indoors, and I recovered enough for Jacqueline to take me to Amsterdam for a five-day holiday. This was the first time I'd been abroad since 1961 and, of course, I could see a little back then.

Alvin looked after Brandy, as I couldn't take her with me due to the quarantine regulations. It seemed so strange not having Brandy with me and, for the first time in her life, Jacqueline had to guide me everywhere. We got on so well that in October we went to Majorca for the first time.

My vet, Mr Downs, thought it was very unfair that we couldn't take our guide dogs abroad, so then started another campaign, to get the quarantine regulations changed.

A new invention came out in this year - a talking reading machine. It was the size of a washing machine and cost £44,000. The machine was shown in the Chelmsford Library and I was filmed by Anglia television, together with Brandy of course. The Kurzweil scanner, as it was called, was like a photocopier, but instead of making another copy of a document it scanned it and then converted it into synthetic speech.

We bought our first caravan at Point Clear in the June, which we kept for 12 years until we bought our little bungalow on the sea wall, which we still have. With no pavements it was quite difficult for Brandy to find her way around the caravan park, but as long as there were no stray dogs around she was fine.

The year ended with me completing 18 talks, Jacqueline turning 21, and Alvin and I getting engaged at Christmas.

1986

Although Brandy was still working well as my guide dog, I was still having a lot of trouble with her going for other dogs.

The final straw came at the start of the year, when I was waiting for a train at Chalkwell station. Brandy saw a dog on the opposite platform, and how she didn't pull me onto the track I'll never know.

After that experience the GDBA decided to take her back to the new Redbridge training centre, which had just opened, so that

51

she could be assessed for a couple of weeks. While she was there, my mum took me for a holiday to Guernsey. On my return, Pete Smith, one of the new trainers, came to see me and told me that they would have to retire Brandy as a guide dog. He explained that, just like a person who's been mugged, due to that initial attack Brandy would always be on her guard. The really sad part was that they wouldn't let me keep her as a pet, as she could upset my new guide dog.

It was arranged for Brandy to go back to the family of her puppy walker in Solihull. When they came to collect her it just broke my heart. This parting was worse than when my Topsy died. I never ever saw Brandy again, and I only heard about her a year after she'd died. I will never let another guide dog go again, even if it means not having a dog for a year.

Although I'd only had Brandy for three years, she had accompanied me on some very important journeys in my life: to Buckingham Palace for my MBE, even though she wasn't allowed in; to the launch of the tactile paving in Parliament Square; to the first meeting of the Access Committee for England; to the launch of the first talking reading machine; and, most importantly of all, comforting me through my divorce and all the events around that year.

No one that is sighted can really understand the relationship between a blind person and their guide dog. We are trained to talk to our dogs all the time when they're working, but I talk to my dog all the time even indoors, as she's my best friend and normally the only one in the house with me. Of course, like me, when she's in her bed she's resting or sleeping and I don't disturb her.

I was so pleased when my publisher, Chris Cowlin, chose Brandy's picture for the front cover of my autobiography, *Just Jill*.

CHAPTER 9
QUELLA

1986

While I still had Brandy, Pete Smith brought Quella, a large black Labrador, to see me. I went for a walk with her round the block to see what I thought. As she was as large as Bunty, I was a little worried. However, Pete assured me that, despite her size, she was a totally different dog. While walking round the block she came to a halt at one point and Pete told me that she'd stopped to look at a man taking photographs across the road. She thought he was taking her picture, as many photos had been taken of her the previous week at Redbridge training centre's official opening, when Quella had been used to demonstrate the obstacles.

Quella had already been out as a guide dog with someone else, who for some reason didn't take to her. Pete thought she would be the right dog for me, however, and he was right.

So on 1 June, the day after Brandy left, I travelled to the new Redbridge centre in Essex, which was a lot nearer to home than Leamington Spa. When I arrived at Redbridge I was still very upset over losing Brandy, but I tried to cheer up as soon as I was given Quella. As she'd already had an unsuccessful guide dog placement, she was already 26 months old. She was more of a stately dog -very slow but very steady, and in control of me completely. She was always obedient and wanted to do everything right. I could never hurry her to get a bus or a train; Quella went at her own speed. This was good for me, as she made me slow down my very busy lifestyle.

Although the training was roughly the same as it was at Leamington, as it was a new establishment I had to start from scratch in terms of finding my way around the building and the outside areas, which took quite some time. However, we finished our training in three weeks instead of the usual four, which was good because I was due to be presented with a £2,450 cheque for the GDBA on 22 June from Trinity Football Club. An old friend from my college days, David Bright, had organised this fundraising for guide dogs and at that time was working as a CID officer in the police force.

Once home, I did two school talks followed by an address at Lampeter University in Wales for the Diamond Jubilee of the Wales Council for the Blind. Barbara came with me for the journey to Wales, as it was too soon for Quella, as a new dog, to embark on such a long journey so soon after training. This journey was a bit hair-raising. We travelled by train to Cardiff and then had to get a taxi. I thought the driver was acting a bit mad, and when we arrived Barbara told me he'd been swigging a can of beer all the way. We did arrive safely, fortunately.

Then, on 31 July, we went off to Woodham Ferris to protest about a level crossing that had been installed without any barriers. I had visited many dangerous railway level crossings throughout the country, one being in Sawbridgeworth, which many blind people living nearby were finding impossible to use on their own.

In September Quella and I travelled to Exeter in Devon to attend a public inquiry, at which I would be speaking. This was to stop a cycle track being built on a pavement that was used by a large number of pedestrians, including blind people.

By this time my guide dogs were being trained to go to the toilet in the gutter. This was easier than with my previous dogs, Topsy,

TOPSY

Topsy, November 1971

With Topsy, Christmas 1980

With Topsy, November 1971

BUNTY

Road research laboratory, 1982

BRANDY

A great photo of Brandy, 1983

BRANDY

With Mick Allen and my daughter
Jaqueline, outside The Palace,
February 1983

Outside The Palace with Brady
with my MBE, February 1983

QUELLA

With Quella in Chelmsford, August 1987

With Alvin, Fabian and Quella

With Quella, Redbridge, 1986

LADY

Success in persuading the management of 'The Royals',
Southend on Sea, to install an automatic door

On a plane to Majorca, March 2003

Spending quality time with Lady

AMANDA

At the House of Commons with Richard Leaman.
Holding a copy of my autobiography 'just Jill', March 2010

AMANDA

In my front garden, March 2010

With Amanda at Chalkwell, July 2011

Bunty and Brandy, who would only go on grass.

In addition to these many journeys I was able to do 33 talks this year with Brandy and Quella.

1987

Alvin and I got married on 10 January, and our guide dogs walked down the aisle alongside us. By this time Alvin had a new guide dog called Otis, a curly-coated retriever. We'd invited Pete Smith, Quella's trainer, to the ceremony and he arrived late. We were walking towards the altar when he appeared and Quella spotted him, so she was wagging her tail as we walked. Otis and Quella both lay still throughout the ceremony.

We were going to Majorca for our honeymoon and couldn't take the dogs, so a friend called Rhona looked after both of them for the week we were away. Alvin had never been abroad, and because his sight was still very bad our friends Barbara and John came as our sighted guides. We didn't really like leaving the dogs, but it does do them good to have a break from us.

As soon as we got back I was busy going to meetings and giving talks. Quella was still working very well and never gave me any problems.

My first event was lunch with a reporter from our local newspaper, *The Yellow Advertiser*, as a local restaurant was going to introduce Braille menus. It was quite funny, as the Braille menu I was given turned out to be a Christmas one. The lunch was good, and it was a great opportunity to show how well a guide dog will behave in a busy restaurant, sitting quietly under the table and not pestering for food. It also gave great publicity, highlighting the usefulness of Braille menus.

A few days later we went to Cranfield in Bedfordshire to attend a conference about the design of buses. The Department of

Transport was trying to encourage bus manufacturers to incorporate the needs of disabled people in their bus designs and make them accessible for all. It was recommended that the new design should have a low-floor entrance, good lighting, colour-contrasted handrails, low bell-pushes and audible announcements. We also needed a space where a guide dog could lie down without being trodden on. In addition, it was important for drivers to undergo disability awareness training.

I only had time to do 23 talks this year. However, on top of my honeymoon in Majorca, Jacqueline took me to Tenerife and Lanzarote.

1988

Every year I'd attended the Liberal Party conference, but this year there was a special conference for the merger with the Social Democrats, which was held in January at Blackpool. There were only 13 speakers, and I was lucky enough to be one of those called to speak. My entire speech was broadcast live on television, and Quella sat quietly by my side throughout.

September was the most important month of the year. Jacqueline moved into her flat in Leigh with her boyfriend Mike on 2 September, and on 14 September I was invited to attend the first European Women's conference in Italy, where I spoke about my experiences of being a blind housewife and mother. At that time, although I was a member of the RNIB Council, there were no women on the International Committee, so chairman Sir John Wall had asked me to go. From that time on I was a member of the International Committee, and gradually other women were elected as members.

After the conference in Italy a Women's Commission was formed in 1990, and I became its vice-chairperson. I was still campaigning to have the quarantine regulations changed so that I could take my guide dog with me.

When Jacqueline moved out she left her cat, Buttons, behind for me to look after. Each time Alvin or I brought home a new dog, on the first night he would sit on top of the television just staring at them. He'd grown up with the dogs from a kitten, and guide dogs are trained with cats at the training centre, so they all got on well together. We used to have to feed Buttons on top of a cupboard, because if we left the food on the floor one of the dogs would pinch it.

One of the ministers I would meet from time to time was Sir Nicholas Scott, who was Minister for Disabled People. One day he invited me to lunch, but I think it was Quella he really wanted to meet. He was very fond of Quella and kept a picture of her on his desk.

A month after that lunch I was in the finals for the Women of the Year awards and enjoyed another very nice lunch at the Savoy Hotel in London. Princess Margaret was the guest of honour, and it was a great honour for me to be able to meet and talk to her. And, of course, Quella got a pat from the Princess. Quella was provided with a large silver bucket filled with drinking water.

I'd been very lucky since becoming blind not to have had any major accidents. I'd had the odd bump on the head from a half-open door or a trip on a cracked pavement, but nothing serious. That was until November of this year. I was carrying Buttons down the stairs and I slipped and fell, hitting the radiator at the bottom. The doctor was called, but he said I'd just cracked my ribs and didn't have to go to hospital. After that I arranged for another handrail to be fitted on my stairs, and I'm a lot more careful now when negotiating them.

Quella and I did another 24 talks this year. One of the schools

I visited was Stambridge School, where I'd been with all my five guide dogs. The children had raised hundreds of pounds to pay for the training of many guide dogs. It was sad when I went with my old guide dog, but they knew I'd be back one day with a new dog. This taught them that a dog's life is relatively short and this was why money had to be raised continually, for the training of new guide dogs.

We also visited my old school, King John's in Benfleet, every day for a week, as the children were involved in a big fund-raising project. That week they raised thousands of pounds, and I returned to present them with framed pictures of dogs that had qualified as guide dogs.

1989

My house, bought back in 1963, had a very small kitchen of about 8ft square. The cooker was located on one wall and the sink on another. This had always made it quite difficult when moving hot saucepans from the cooker across to the sink, so Alvin and I decided to have an extension built.

The extension was completed in January and included the installation of a new central heating gas boiler and a back door leading from the kitchen into a 10ft dog run where the dogs could go to the toilet, as well as a water supply with a tap and hose so that the run could be cleaned.

We also had a toilet added next to our dining room, which turned out to be a blessing when my mum had her leg amputated in 1990 and came to stay with us every weekend.

In April Alvin and I went to Majorca on our own for the first time, as Barbara and John, who had accompanied us twice in the past, were going to become Mayor and Mayoress of Southend in May. We still couldn't take our guide dogs with us, as the quarantine regulations hadn't been changed.

On 12 July we opened another branch of the NFB in Southend, which gave guide dog owners the opportunity to meet as well as helping those people losing their sight.

It was the 100th anniversary of Southend Pier, the longest pier in the world, on 7 August and we all (apart from Quella) dressed up in Victorian costume. Quella took a very active part in the celebrations on the pier, together with our friends Barbara and John, who were now Mayor and Mayoress.

Rhona, who had looked after our guide dogs while we went to Majorca, was married in September, and I made her wedding cake for her.

Also in September Quella and I were invited to have lunch with Nicholas Scott, Minister for the Disabled. By this time guide dogs were allowed into the public gallery of the House of Commons. While we sat and listened to the debate about discrimination, in his speech Nicholas Scott referred to his four-legged friend in the public gallery, giving examples of the access problems I'd experienced over many years, including with the House itself.

We did 24 talks this year, including a few at the local Southend Hospital, where I was born in 1940 and where many members of my family had died. I would train all levels of staff how to guide a blind person and serve food and drinks, and would make them aware of all the needs that a blind person has while either visiting a hospital as an out-patient or staying as an in-patient. I also highlighted the need for correspondence to be made available in large print, in Braille and on audio. I told them that guide dogs should be allowed to accompany their owners for out-patient appointments, although they would probably need a friend or family member to look after the dog if hospitalised. I taught the staff not to talk to a guide dog while it was working and to never feed it, although offering a bowl of water might be helpful, with the permission of the owner.

I know of many instances where blind people haven't been aware that food has been left on a tray or table in front of them, or that the tea trolley has gone by. This has happened to me countless times on a train. My guide dog cannot let me know, and I try to listen carefully so that I can call out, "Is that the tea trolley?"

The most exciting event of the year was when my daughter Jacqueline got engaged to her long-term boyfriend Mike in November.

1990

The year started with the usual talks to schools, and then on 22 January we attended a demonstration in Whitehall, campaigning for a law to stop discrimination against disabled people.

In February my mum was very ill with the flu, but due to an ambulance strike she couldn't be taken to hospital. By the time an ambulance was available to take her, it was too late. On her 75th birthday she had to have her whole leg amputated. This was a very difficult time for me, and Quella was so good, coping with all these extra journeys to and from the hospital.

In the March I was going to turn 50, and in the November Jacqueline would be 25, so we'd planned to have a joint party at the church. However, as my mum was so ill in hospital, we just had an open house party at home. Relatives and friends did visit my mum, but it was very difficult for them all.

Jacqueline and Mike's wedding was booked for 30 June, and we were anxious that my mum got herself well enough to attend the ceremony. On the day we were able to get her to the service in a wheelchair, although she was still very ill.

While all this was going on, Alvin's guide dog Otis died quite suddenly, even though he was only five years old. So Alvin had to go off to Redbridge again to get another dog and came home with a black retriever cross called Fabian. He was like a teddy bear, and Quella and Fabian got on very well together.

In the April Quella and I travelled to Liverpool by train to attend the National Consumer Congress at the university. It was my second visit there. The previous time I'd been with Topsy, and the fire alarms had gone off at 3 o'clock in the morning. At the training centre we'd been trained in what to do in this situation, so I just followed the procedure and put on my coat and shoes, then the dog's lead and harness, before exiting the room. As we began walking down the corridor, the other delegates asked me if I was all right. I hadn't realised that the lights weren't working, so I told all the other delegates to follow me and Topsy. We led them down three flights of stairs to the ground floor.

As it turned out, there wasn't a fire, but it was good practice and illustrated that a blind person can be of help in such a situation. Some places used emergency evacuation as an excuse not to allow blind people into their premises.

In the same month we had another meeting with Nicholas Scott, Minister for the Disabled, and we also attended the official opening of the RNIB's distribution centre at Peterborough, which was carried out by David Blunkett MP.

In May we went to speak at another public inquiry, this time in Taunton in Somerset, relating to another proposed shared facility for cyclists and pedestrians.

I went to Ireland for the first time in May, flying from Stansted to Dublin. Quella treated the plane just like a bus. It was very small and the floor must've been uncomfortable for her. I was speaking at a conference about the access needs of blind people.

In June I organised a conference for the NFB's Environment Committee, which was held at the RNIB HQ in London, and Cecil Parkinson, Minister for Transport, came to open it for me.

Alvin and I were also able to go to Majorca for the second time on our own. We still couldn't take the dogs, so they were looked after for the first time by Fabian's puppy walkers, Carol and Stewart. Quella's puppy walkers lived in Reading, so they were too far away to help us.

That the puppy walkers can take care of our dogs from time to time is great for both parties. Puppy walkers look after prospective guide dogs from the age of around 7 weeks until they're about 12 months old, when they first start their training, so it's nice for them to see the dogs again and we know they're in safe, known hands.

Even in this busy year, we still fitted in 22 talks and lots of meetings.

1991

January started with a visit to Paris. I went to the conference as a representative of the Department of Transport's Advisory Committee (DPTAC), and it marked the start of a campaign for air regulations that would enable disabled people to travel by air with all the help they required and stop discrimination against people with reduced mobility. This, of course, included those of us with guide dogs, as our dogs weren't allowed to fly with us to locations outside of the UK. It took until 2008 for these new regulations to be passed by the European Parliament.

In March I organised a conference for the NFB at Birmingham Airport. The manager at the time was a fellow member of the DPTAC, so he allowed us to use his conference hall. Nicholas

Scott, Minister for the Disabled, opened the conference, which covered all aspects of our Environment Committee's work.

For about three years I'd been on a planning group as a representative of the DPTAC, to help with the design of Stansted Airport, and on 15 February Her Majesty the Queen came to open the new building.

Unfortunately, it was not until 2010 that guide dogs were allowed to fly from that airport out of the country, which meant that Quella could never come on holiday to Majorca with us. She did make many flights within the UK, however, as we used to fly to various airports to check out their access facilities on behalf of the DPTAC.

I was invited to speak at a conference about the Street Works Act, held at the International Conference Centre in Birmingham, which was attended by 900 delegates.

In November our local Palace Theatre was the second theatre in the country to introduce audio-described shows, where the blind person would wear a headset and someone would describe all the non-dialogue sections, plus the scenery and costumes.

There was never any problem taking guide dogs into the theatres in Southend, but the cinemas wouldn't allow access, which meant that I could never take Jacqueline to the cinema when she was a child. Instead, my husband had to take her, while I stayed at home with my dog.

On 1 August a new neighbour called Lily came to help me for the first time. Unfortunately, she was really frightened of dogs, but after a few weeks she got used to Quella lying in my office while she read the post to me. Gradually Lily built up the confidence to give her a little pat. Fortunately, Quella was a very gentle dog, whereas some dogs want to jump up, which can be particularly frightening for children.

In September I retired as a member of the Access Committee for England after seven years' service, and I was appointed to the new Disability Living Allowance Board by Nicholas Scott, now Minister for Social Security. I was also appointed shortly afterwards to the Independent Tribunal Service, which helped those that had been turned down for the Disability Living Allowance. This meant that Quella had to learn two new routes in her later life, as well as the layout of a new building, but she coped very well.

As well as another 23 talks this year, we were honoured to be invited to a lunch to celebrate Ann Frye's OBE. Ann had been responsible for setting up the DPTAC committee at the Department of Transport and was head of the mobility unit. Ann had supported me in all our campaigns about access for guide dogs and other pavement and transport matters.

1992

The NFB had been running the 'Give Us Back Our Pavements' campaign since 1978, using leaflets and posters paid for by the local Access credit card company. However, we needed to have a video made, and we were very pleased when the GDBA gave us enough money for this to be done.

The filming took place in the streets close to my house, and Tony Robinson did the narration. Quella taking me to Coventry to meet Tony Robinson also featured in the video, which was called *Get Streetwise*. It was first shown in Lyon, France, at a conference organised by the Department of Transport, and it was officially launched in the UK by Roger Freeman, Minister for Transport, on 8 June.

A couple of weeks later we went to the Isle of Man, so that I could talk to the Manx Government and show them the video.

Alvin, Barbara and John accompanied Quella and me on this four-day trip, and we flew from Stansted on a very small plane.

On 24 September I was presented with the Ratcliffe Award at the Mobility Road Show.

My mum went into hospital on 9 July and stayed there until she died on 19 October. She had struggled for three years with her leg amputation and she'd had no quality of life. Just before she died she knew that Jacqueline and Mike were expecting a baby and that I was going to be President of the NFB.

For those four months that my mum was in Southend Hospital, Quella guided me there nearly every day, although occasionally I was taken by car. It was one place that I'd never experienced problems with access, and yet it wouldn't have surprised me if I'd been refused entry by such an establishment. Even when my dad was in intensive care, the hospital phoned me and said if I had no one to bring me and I needed my dog to take me there, they would look after her outside the door.

On 29 October, just ten days after my mother passed away, I accompanied my Uncle Bernard, my dad's brother, to Buckingham Palace to receive an MBE for his 40 years' voluntary work for the Lifeboats Service. On this occasion I didn't even ask if I could take Quella and just went with my cousin and uncle.

In this very emotional year I was only able to fit in 20 talks to schools and other groups, and it ended with a welcome two-week holiday in Majorca.

1993

The most important event of this year was the birth of my grandson, Joseph, in May.

Also I'd been elected as the first female NFB President and I chaired my first conference in Aberdeen, Scotland, in October. Quella and I flew from Gatwick to Aberdeen, as it was cheaper and quicker than going by train.

At this conference we usually had about 12 guide dogs, all well behaved. Whenever we booked a hotel for a conference we always had to make sure that there were suitable facilities for our guide dogs to go to the toilet. So long as they'd had their food, a short walk and the chance to go to the toilet, they were quite happy to sleep under the conference tables. Some do snore, of course, and occasionally one might give a bark, just to join in with the clapping.

1994

Although Quella was only ten-and-a-half and very fit, because she was a very slow dog and had a few grey hairs it was decided to retire her as a guide dog. After the trauma of parting with Brandy, I said I wanted to keep her as a pet and this was agreed.

However, when a guide dog retires but remains in the household and you get a new guide dog, you aren't allowed to take them both out together. So many of my friends would come round to take Quella out. Also, Alvin still had his guide dog Fabian, even though he'd had corneal grafts by then and could see a little better, so he would take the two dogs to the park on leads most days.

This kept Quella very fit, and she lived until she was fifteen-and-a-half. Over the 13 years that I'd had her, we were filmed many times, and she was always ready to sit and in her own way smile at the cameras.

CHAPTER 10
LADY

1995

I went to Redbridge for training with my fifth guide dog, Lady, on 1 June. Lady was only 17 months old and was a very lively black Labrador, very much like Topsy. We got through our training in two-and-a-half weeks.

Her trainer was a young girl called Charlie, who had taught Lady to jump up at traffic lights to show me the location of the press button. When she first did this I was horrified and told her off, as we'd been taught that guide dogs should always keep their four feet on the ground and shouldn't jump up at people or onto furniture, etc. In discussion with the older trainers at the centre, it was decided that this wasn't a safe way to behave at a crossing. What I did let Lady do, however, was jump up and place her two front paws on the desk at a station booking office or at a hotel reception. It certainly helped to make a positive identification of the correct location, but I wouldn't do it again with another dog, as I think that this is what led to Lady developing arthritis in her back legs when she was only nine years old.

It was my third year as President of the NFB, and the first meeting that Lady and I attended was at Richmond House in Whitehall, London, with the then Minister for the Disabled, William Hague, and Colin Low, CBE. The meeting was about the proposed Disability Discrimination bill that was going through Parliament and didn't include transport and education, so Colin and I were there to change the Minister's mind, which we did.

Lady, like Quella and Topsy, worked very well and she quickly learnt her routes to the station and to the shops, as well as her way around the London underground.

The last conference I had to chair as President of the NFB was at the Swallow Hotel, Gateshead. Lady and I flew to Newcastle airport, where she'd already been during her training. Jacqueline's second child wasn't due for another ten days, but during the night of 5 October Mike phoned to tell me that Jacqueline had gone into labour. Not surprisingly, I didn't sleep much. It was about 4 a.m. when Mike phoned again to tell me I had a granddaughter called Emily Rose. I was so excited and found it quite difficult to start chairing the conference at 9 a.m.

Although I attended many meetings this year, I didn't have time to fit in any talks.

1996

During 1996 the Disability Discrimination Act (DDA), for which we had all fought so hard for over many years, was passed. This would hopefully stop people refusing to allow guide dogs in taxis, hotels, restaurants and other places where I'd been denied access with my own guide dogs over the previous 26 years.

This Act also aimed to improve access to public buildings, and one success for me was as Secretary of the Southend Access Committee. I wrote to the Royals Shopping Centre, requesting that they install automatic doors at the entrances. I was really surprised when, after just that one letter explaining their duty under the new Act, they agreed and these doors were fitted at a cost of £10,000.

The NFB had its annual delegates conference in Wigan, and it was there that I met Peter Wilkins. Peter came from Stockport and he didn't have a guide dog, as he had been born blind and had trained himself to get around with a white cane. The following year we would start work together on European issues.

Although I'd finished my three years as President of the NFB, I went back to being Public Relations Officer again.

Now that the DDA was in force, Lady and I took plenty of opportunities to test out the new Act. Even though taxis should not refuse us, they weren't stopping to pick us up when I held up my 'TAXI' card just because they saw my dog, which was very annoying. I knew this was happening, as sometimes a sighted person would tell me that a taxi had just gone past and the driver was pointing at my dog. As I couldn't see to take their number, however, I couldn't report them.

On one occasion I was waiting for a taxi in the Euston Road in London. It was dark at the time and a passer-by helped me to hail a black cab. I got in and told the driver my destination, and then he started to chat to me, asking the usual questions:

"How long have you been blind?"

"What caused it?"

Then he said, "Why don't you have a guide dog?"

I replied, "I do have one. She's lying here with me."

He was really shocked, and then told me that he didn't take dogs of any kind. After explaining the law to him, I asked him why he wouldn't normally carry a dog. His response was that he thought they might go to the toilet in the taxi and climb on the seats. By the time we'd finished the 25-minute journey to Fenchurch Street station I think he'd learnt a thing or two.

Following that journey I submitted an article to the taxi trade magazine.

1997

We had big changes in our family this year. My daughter Jacqueline, her husband Mike and my grandchild Joseph moved to Hampshire in August, as my son-in-law changed his place of employment. This meant frequent journeys for Lady and I to Southampton, which involved the usual half-hour walk to Chalkwell station, the 50-minute train ride to Fenchurch Street station and then a 15-minute taxi ride to Waterloo, where I caught the train to Southampton Central, a journey of around 90 minutes. Jacqueline would meet me in her car at the station.

I was delighted when the Jubilee line was built on the underground, but after using it three times I went back to expensive taxis, due to the lack of staff to help me at West Ham station. Over the years I've witnessed a real reduction in staff numbers at railway stations. In fact, my own mother stopped using trains because of the lack of staff to help her.

In November Alvin and I sold our caravan at Point Clear and bought a little bungalow that was situated right on the sea wall there. In actual fact, we didn't really sell our caravan. It was just taken off the site by the company that owns the caravan park, as we hadn't paid the ground rent for the following year due to our negotiations to buy the bungalow, and we didn't get a penny for it.

I was able to take Quella and Lady together down to the bungalow. Friends would take us by car, and I was able to take both of the dogs for walks along the sea wall, where there was plenty of grass that provided a safe area for them to have a run.

It was also in 1997 that I was elected by the European Blind Union (EBU) board to chair the Commission on Mobility and Guide Dogs. Our first meeting was in Prague, but of course I couldn't take Lady due to the unchanged quarantine regulations. However, a new campaign group, Passports for Pets, had been set up by Lady Mary Fretwell, and she actually used to look after Lady for me while I went abroad. She thought it was so unfair that I couldn't take my dog with me.

The Eurostar train had started to run under the English Channel, and because the quarantine regulations were going to be relaxed the GDBA asked me and Lady to spend a day on the Eurostar train from Waterloo to the tunnel to practise the evacuation procedure in the case of an emergency. Alvin came with us. When the train stopped in a tunnel and we had to get off, we walked to the front of the train and then Alvin had to lift Lady off as the gap was too wide for her to jump. We then had to walk along a narrow footpath to a safety area. We were given a packed lunch, which we enjoyed while sitting in our first-class seats. Lady and I both got a certificate for taking part.

1998

Lady was now four years old and Quella was fourteen but still very well for her age. As I was now making more trips abroad and fitting in holidays in Majorca and visits to the bungalow at Point Clear, Lady was working very hard and I wasn't spending so much time with Quella. However, she was never left alone. Alvin would often take her to his music shop, where she would lie in her bed, and sometimes friends would pop by and take her out for a short walk. In fact, we had a little ramp made for her to help her get into cars, as her back legs were getting weak.

Following the success of the *Get Streetwise* video launched in 1994, the NFB decided to make another video. This one was called *Eye Spy Help*, and its aim was to provide information to people that were going blind and didn't know where to go for help.

Lady and I started to give talks in the Clacton area, where our bungalow was situated, visiting Brownies and Beavers clubs and local schools.

We also made a long trip to Bridgend in Wales this year. Lady had been puppy-walked by a lady from Wales called Rose Hunter, who'd actually taught her some Welsh commands. So when Rose came to visit us one day at home, she told Lady to sit and stay in Welsh, and she did. I'd just had a meeting with one of the government ministers, who seemed to think that blindness wasn't a severe disability and that, as I had a guide dog, I should be completely independent. I had to explain to him that guide dogs couldn't read, write or talk, which was why blind people needed help from sighted people, for instance to read the post, fill in forms, read bus and train timetables, or inform you what bus number was coming.

In June Peter Wilkins made his first visit abroad, accompanying Barbara and I to Helsinki, Finland, for our EBU Commission meeting.

In July I made my first long-haul flight, to Atlanta, for the International Mobility conference. An old friend from college, Betty Harper, came with me as my guide. This was followed in September by a longer flight to Perth, in Australia.

On my return I travelled to Southampton with Lady for my granddaughter's third birthday, which involved carrying on the train journey the cake I'd made for her. From there we went on to a Braille conference in Cardiff.

We completed our very busy year in London, where we hosted another EBU Commission meeting, which was the first time that the members of my Commission had been able to meet Lady due to the quarantine laws. This time, those travelling from abroad to the UK experienced the same problem and had to leave their guide dogs at home.

1999

The RNIB gave 'See It Right' awards each year, and I was really pleased when my neighbour Lily became a recipient. I had nominated her for helping me every day over a period of eight years. Lily came over every evening and read my post to me, and she would fill out all my expense claims. As all the work I did was voluntary, I was spending hundreds of pounds each month on train and taxi fares, and a form had to be completed for each claim, with relevant receipts attached. Lily was the one that didn't really like dogs, but she was now used to having Lady at her feet in my office.

On 9 June the *Eye Spy Help* video was launched by David Blunkett MP, the then Secretary of State for Education and also a guide dog owner.

Two months later came one of the saddest days of my life. On 31 August Quella had to be put to sleep. She was 15 years and 4 months old, which was a very good age for a Labrador. My friend Moira drove Alvin, Quella and I to the vet's, where I stayed with Quella while she was put to sleep. Lady and Alvin's dog Fabian were left at home.

It was only another month later when Fabian was diagnosed with cancer and had to be put to sleep as well.

My poor Lady really pined for her two playmates and was quite lonely with out them, after being together for four years. Alvin didn't need another guide dog, as his corneal grafts had restored enough vision for him not to need a dog.

In September one of my two godsons got married in Derby and, as the NFB conference was the same weekend in Hull, Lady and I had a very long, tiring journey from Hull to Derby and back in a single day.

The EBU General Assembly, which was held every four years, took place in Prague, and there I was re-elected to chair the Commission on Mobility and Guide Dogs. This time they changed the name to cover transport as well as mobility and guide dog matters.

Our holidays this year included our first visit to Cyprus and our first time staying at the Carla Blanca in Majorca, which became our regular accommodation from now on. We had been going to Majorca every year since 1985 and had previously stayed at the Santa Lucia and the San Matias.

We managed to fit in six talks this year.

We had a sad ending to the year when my Uncle Bernard, who'd been like a father to me since the death of my dad in 1978, was admitted to Southend Hospital and spent the whole of Christmas and New Year there. With no bus service to the hospital, it was a half-hour walk each way for Lady and me to visit him.

2000

We were due to go to Majorca at the beginning of January, but on our departure day Alvin was taken ill and he had to spend a week in hospital. We thought he was having a heart attack at the time, but it turned out that he was very anaemic and needed a blood transfusion.

Uncle Bernard was still in hospital, so Lady and I found ourselves going from one ward to the other. We eventually got to Majorca in February.

In March I celebrated my 60th birthday with a party at home and a meal out with friends. Lady was now six years old and still keeping well.

Uncle Bernard died in July, at the age of 85, which was a great loss in my life.

In November I made my second visit to Australia, for the World Blind Union's conference. When I first arrived in the conference

74

room, one of the helpers came over to say hello to me. I didn't recognise his voice due to the Australian twang, but as soon as he told me his name, Mark Fisher, I was so thrilled, as he'd been Brandy's trainer back in 1983. He hadn't heard what had happened to her, so he was obviously upset when I told him. Mark was now working at Melbourne's guide dog training centre.

I also went to Belgium and France for EBU meetings, and in December I went to Prague with Peter and Barbara, where a talking information system is used on all the buses, trams and trains. Even though a guide dog can find the right bus stop or train platform and guide you on and off a bus or train, you have to rely on the announcements to tell you the destination and, once on board, you need to know where you are on the journey so that you can prepare to get off the vehicle at the appropriate time. The system in Prague is excellent and, as well as being used on public transport vehicles, it is also employed in some public buildings.

2001

This year we continued with our talks and meetings, and after 30 years I decided to stand down as a member of the NFB's Executive Council. I still carried on chairing the Environment Committee and continued my role as Public Relations Officer, and I was still a member of the RNIB Council.

Jacqueline came with me for the first time to one of my EBU meetings, held in Norway, and Lily joined Lady and me for a week's holiday in Eastbourne.

The last meeting of the year was in Denmark and was held in a purpose-built building for blind people. It even had sheepskin rugs for the guide dogs to lie on. All the bedrooms were on the ground floor and each led outside to a little enclosed garden where the dogs could go to the toilet.

It was quite similar to my experiences back in 1974, when I organised a conference in Southend for the Circle of Guide Dog Owners and we used the Southend Airport Hotel. This hotel had small chalets in the grounds with their own little gardens.

Most hotels never think of making such areas for dogs and tend to focus on provision for cars instead. It would be so cheap and easy for toilet facilities to be created for guide dogs in car parks or at railway and bus stations, simply by fencing off a 10ft area. It's getting increasingly difficult to find places for this necessity.

2002

I'd been going to Eastbourne for many years, to the RNIB's hotel, Palm Court. However, in January I decided to host a rock n' roll weekend there, which was so successful that another one was held the following year. Then the hotel was sold, so we had to move the event to the Albany Lyons Hotel on the seafront at Eastbourne.

The Palm Court was the venue for the NFB's annual delegates conference in September, which was attended by 60 blind people and about 12 guide dogs.

Lady and I then went to a conference in Cardiff in February, organised by Voice of the Listener and Viewer (VLV). I'd represented the NFB on VLV for many years, and it gave me the opportunity to listen to and question radio and television directors, managers, programme makers and the chairman of the BBC. Usually these meetings were held every six months in London, but sometimes additional meetings and conferences were organised in other parts of the country.

After returning from Cardiff Lady and I travelled to Manchester to attend the Liberal Democrats' spring conference. It was my birthday weekend and I was able to spend it with my friend Peter, who lives in Stockport. Lady and I then had a very long train journey straight to my daughter's home in Southampton, where we stayed for a few days before returning home.

In September Lady and I were due to go to a conference in Liverpool on our own. It was a Monday morning and it was pouring with rain. We left home at 7 a.m. and arrived at Euston station dripping wet. Very quickly a member of staff took us to the first coach of the train, which turned out to be the first-class carriage. While I was trying to dry both myself and Lady, a man offered to help me. I thanked him, but told him that we were okay. He sat and chatted to me for the three-hour journey to Liverpool, and it was only after about an hour that I found out who was talking to me. It was Holly Johnson, the lead singer of Frankie Goes to Hollywood.

On one of our journeys to Southampton Lady had her first accident. We were getting on the train at Waterloo station when she slipped between the platform and the train and fell onto the track, with me still holding her lead. The member of staff with me radioed to the driver of the train. All the power was switched off and an announcement was made that there was a dog on the track. The driver came, took Lady's lead and guided her to the back of the train, where he was able to lift her back onto the platform. The staff then got out the wheelchair ramps to make it easier for Lady to get on the train. The ramps were used again on our arrival at Southampton, and from then on this was the procedure every time I travelled with Lady.

After a visit to the vet I found out that Lady had arthritis in her back legs, even though she was only nine years old, and this explained why she'd fallen. The vet assured me that she wasn't in pain and could carry on working, but he recommended that we used lifts wherever possible rather than stairs and didn't embark on too many long walks.

Lady had a very different tail to my other four dogs. Hers was always sticking up and wagging. She was a very happy dog and loved working, so it was quite hard to change our working pattern. I actually put on about three stone in weight over the following two years, just because I wasn't using the stairs at stations or walking so much.

We only did two local talks this year, but we'd attended many meetings in different parts of the country.

As a result of Lady's accident, I learnt to say thank you more often. I wrote to Waterloo station to thank them for helping me that day when Lady had fallen, and they wrote back to thank me for thanking them. People often complain, but very few say thank you, so from that day on I tried to thank someone each week, either with a card or a gift.

2003

I was going to be 63 this year and so I decided that I must write my autobiography, which I started on 1 January. I only had a talking typewriter then, so I had to type it and then get my daughter to transfer it onto a computer.

The quarantine regulations had been changed, so for the first time I was able to take Lady with me to Majorca in March. She had to have a rabies vaccination and a blood test to make sure she was fit to travel and then I received her Pet Passport.

The only airline that would take us was British Midland, which meant we had to travel to Heathrow for our flight. Alvin and Lily came too, and while we were waiting in the departure lounge the captain came to see us and said, "We'll upgrade you to first class, as there'll be more room for the dog." Lady just curled up at my feet as though it was a bus or train. During the flight the captain came to check that Lady was all right. She just slept all the way.

The manager of the Carla Blanca was so pleased to welcome Lady and told me she was the best behaved guest he'd had. We took her food with us, together with a blanket, her brush and comb, and a toy. She very quickly learnt her way around Palma Nova, and all the shopkeepers were really happy to see her. We'd been going there without my guide dog for 18 years, so all the friends we'd made were very pleased to meet Lady.

Before returning home we had to go to the vet for Lady to have the required treatment, in compliance with the new regulations.

Once back at home Lady went for her usual six-monthly check-up at the vet's and she was given an injection to help the arthritis in her hips, but I was assured that she wasn't in pain.

On 1 September I attended the first meeting of the new RNIB Assembly, having been elected by the members. Unfortunately the Executive Council, which had been made up of representatives from organisations of blind people, had been disbanded the previous year and had been replaced by an Assembly, which meant that all the committees that I'd attended in London over the past 30 years had gone. This eased the workload for Lady.

In December the EBU held its General Assembly in Athens, which I attended with Betty Harper, and I was re-elected to chair the Commission on Mobility and Transport.

Even though Lady now had her passport, Greece had not yet agreed to allow entry to guide dogs. At that time guide dogs weren't trained for blind people in Greece.

I had to attend quite a few other meetings abroad this year, so I only fitted in six talks, and the year ended with the retirement of

Professor Ian Bruce, Director-General of the RNIB.

2004

We held our Sixties Weekend at Palm Court for the last time in January, as the RNIB's hotel was due to close that year.

In March I turned 64, and we spent our annual holiday in Majorca again, taking Lady for the second time. She had remembered our room and her way around Palma Nova.

If I had remained married to Mick, 6 June would've been our ruby wedding anniversary, and it also marked the 40th anniversary of my going totally blind. I spent the day on my own at my bungalow at Point Clear with Lady. She was really slowing down, but she still enjoyed her walks along the sea wall and having a game with her toys with me. She also liked to lie out in the sun.

On my return we did one of our regular talks to the Brownies at my own church, Chalkwell Park Methodist. The Brownies decided that they would make Christmas cards for me to send to my blind friends every year, each with a tactile picture on it. They, like all children, loved to ask questions about Lady, and at the end of each talk they loved to come and pat her.

Each time I arrived at Clacton station I was always met by a taxi driver called John, so it came as a great shock to me when he died quite suddenly not long after being diagnosed with cancer. John died on the same day that my own dad had died 26 years earlier, and he was so much like my dad. He was very kind and never complained, even when he was in a great deal of pain. His wife, Loraine, has continued to help me over the years.

The rest of the year was spent attending meetings and conferences. The journeys were taking longer now, as Lady was really slowing down.

2005

We started 2005 by holding our Sixties Weekend at the Albany Lyons Hotel in Eastbourne, which was attended by around 90 blind and partially sighted people and 12 guide dogs. It was a much larger hotel than the Palm Court, and it had a lovely large ballroom to accommodate our dancing. As it was positioned on the seafront, the dogs could go out for nice long walks along the promenade, after which they were quite content to sit under the tables while we all danced and sang till late in the evening. Some dogs chose to go to bed in the room.

On 12 January we attended a reception at the House of Lords for the 40th anniversary of Ricability, a charity organisation that assessed equipment and services for the elderly and disabled. I had become a trustee of Ricability a couple of years earlier.

We had our two weeks away in February and Lady came with us, although she'd just had a little tumour removed from her leg. We returned to my 65th birthday party, and as usual I did all the catering myself at home for my 28 friends and family. Over the past year I'd lost three stone in weight, so I was feeling quite fit.

I was due to go to a meeting on 11 July at Surrey University. Before I went, however, my guide dog trainer visited and told me that I must retire Lady as she wasn't really fit enough to work anymore. Obviously I was very upset. I knew that this time would come eventually, but it's that final word and moment that all guide dog owners dread. Lady was 11 years and 8 months old, so she had worked for just over 10 years.

As with Quella, I decided I was going to keep Lady, and I carried on taking her out with me but not working her.

On 4 August Lady came with me by car to BBC Essex, where I was the guest of Steve Scruton on his *Tea at Three* programme. After the broadcast we went to Point Clear for a two-week holiday.

On our return we went to Majorca on our own. Our friends and neighbours had a villa in Majorca and asked me if Lady and I would like to go and stay with them for a fortnight. I'd never dreamt that I would ever fly on my own, and it all happened so quickly.

A taxi took me to Heathrow airport and then I was helped by the staff. Alison and Gordon met me at Palma airport and Lady and I had a lovely, relaxing holiday, which we both needed. Every minute with Lady was very precious, as I knew she wouldn't have too long left to live.

On 5 September poor Lady had to have three lumps removed, as well as a bad tooth. The vet assured me that she was not suffering and she soon recovered once more.

Later that month Tim Howell, a guide dog trainer, brought me a new dog to take a look at. She was a black Labrador called Amanda and she was almost two years old. We had a short walk and talk and, although Amanda seemed to work okay, I was concerned on hearing from the girl with Tim, who had actually trained Amanda, that she hadn't been able to train her to go to the toilet in the gutter. I explained that it was important for my dogs to use the gutter, as I went to many different places where there was no grass or any proper toilet area for dogs. Tim said he would take over the training of Amanda, which he did, and this time the gutter training was successful.

Since my training with Lady at Redbridge the GDBA had closed their training centres, so people were either trained at home or in a hotel. I chose to be trained at home due to my commitments with meetings and overseas trips, and Tim returned on 20 September with Amanda to start training.

CHAPTER 11
AMANDA

2005

Magnus Walker, the centre manager, came to qualify me on 20 October, just two days before Amanda's second birthday.

Training at home was so different to being at a training centre, and I certainly didn't enjoy it as much. I missed the social side and learning alongside and helping new guide dog owners. Also I think everyone learnt a lot from the communal mealtimes, when we sat with different members of staff. It was good for the dogs to be with other dogs, too, both in the minibus and in the evenings spent in the lounge. Although you worked hard whether at home or at a training centre, it certainly seemed more relaxing at a centre, when you were away from daily chores and could focus solely on the training.

Amanda wasn't an easy dog to work with. Like Bunty, she pulled a lot and, like Brandy, she had a lot of dog distraction problems. Unlike Brandy, however, her attitude towards other dogs was loving and kind rather than aggressive, and she just wanted to go and make friends. She also wanted to stop to sniff a lot, which is just what a guide dog shouldn't do when working.

Due to my weight loss I was very fit, and Alvin was used to handling strong guide dogs having had six of his own. So between us we were able to cope with Amanda, and after about 18 months she became a good guide dog.

Mind you, when I worked with Topsy, Quella and Lady I was able to relax so much that I could almost go to sleep, knowing that they would stop at any kerb and take me around any overhanging branches or other obstacle, but with Amanda I had to be on the ball all the time.

One activity on which Amanda scored excellently was her recall in the park. Often I didn't even have to call her, as most days she would be standing beside me waiting for her harness to be put on after our 15-minute walk around the park. Also, on my trips to London, which involve walking past the park on the way to the railway station, she is quite happy to walk past the park without trying to pull me into it after being instructed to head for the station.

Amanda is the only dog I've had that very seldom barks. All the others barked when my doorbell rang or if someone was approaching the gate. The only time Amanda barks is if I accidentally shut her out in the garden.

During this very busy year I had no time to do any talks.

2006

Amanda was still pulling a lot, so my trainer gave her a Halti head collar to wear, but she didn't like it and still managed to stop and sniff, so it wasn't very successful.

On 9 January Lady had a tumour removed from her leg and afterwards had to wear a protector over her head, like a large lampshade, to prevent her from licking her wound. It was very difficult, as she had to wear it at night as well. Luckily, it was only for a few days.

We left Lady with a friend while we went to Eastbourne for our Sixties Weekend. On our return Amanda had her first visit to the House of Commons for a meeting. She was still pulling, but she was well behaved.

The first six months of the year were spent sitting on many tribunal panels in Basildon, Colchester and at Fox Court in

London.

We went to Majorca in March and June, staying with my friend Gill on the first visit and with my friend Betty on the second occasion. Betty lives in Santa Ponza, which wasn't the best of places to take Amanda. She spent most of the time hoovering the pavements.

Amanda, like Lady, watches me packing my case and then getting her bag ready. I weigh out her food into individual meal portions, so all I have to do is empty one bag into her bowl each mealtime. She gets fed twice a day, first thing in the morning and then again at around 4 p.m. Lady was going to stay with friends, so I had to get her things ready too.

We usually get a taxi to the airport, as it's too difficult to cope with a guide dog and all the bags otherwise. Although Alvin has a little vision, it isn't good enough to read all the signs, guide me and carry all the luggage. We always book assistance before we go.

One problem we encounter once we've entered the airport is that there is nowhere for Amanda to go to the toilet, so I have to limit the amount of water she drinks. If it's a morning flight I don't give Amanda her breakfast until we arrive at the hotel. When we arrive at Palma, as soon as we leave the airport building, Amanda goes straight to a little piece of grass outside the doors and spends a penny.

On one occasion, while we were at the check-in desk at Heathrow and Alvin was putting our luggage onto the conveyor belt, Amanda, who was standing next to me, saw her bag, pushed past me and jumped onto the counter! All the staff thought it was funny, but I just told her to get down and behave like a guide dog.

In August we had a collection for a new charity called Seeing

Dogs Alliance, which was set up by a group of guide dog owners. The charity only has one paid member, the trainer of the dogs, and everyone else works on a voluntary basis. We collect postage stamps to help the charity.

On 7 September the vet told me that Lady had cancer and didn't have much longer to live. Then, just a day later, I was taken ill, which stopped me from going to the NFB's annual conference and the Liberal Democrats conference. I think it was just the shock of hearing about Lady, and I soon recovered and got back to my busy life.

On 6 November I was invited to the British Library in London to celebrate Colin Low being made a Lord. Colin had worked with me for the NFB since 1972, and he wrote the Foreword for my autobiography, *Just Jill*. Amanda came with me, and by now she was a lot quieter and not so excitable in the company of other dogs.

On 15 November Lady had her 13th birthday.

On 4 December there was a demonstration in London about the higher rate mobility component of the Disability Living Allowance, which wasn't being paid to blind people, and the following day I spoke at a public inquiry against Southend Council's plans to create a shared footpath for cyclists and pedestrians.

We finished the year carol singing at Fenchurch Street railway station to raise money for the NFB. With Amanda's help we collected £500. Amanda isn't allowed to wear her harness when I'm collecting, so she just lies on a blanket, often rolling on her back to have her tummy rubbed.

Once again we had no time for talks this year.

2007

This year started with our annual Sixties Weekend at

Eastbourne, which Alvin and I organised for about 90 blind and partially sighted people from all over the country.

My first meeting this year was in Brussels, and I travelled there on the Eurostar train. I don't take Amanda with me on such short trips abroad, as it isn't worth the hassle or cost of having to take her to the vet before leaving and before I can return. It's an expense that I can't claim back from anyone. So Amanda stays with Alvin in his music shop and I ask a friend to go with me.

The public inquiry that had started in December the previous year continued. The proposed shared footpath for cyclists and pedestrians was along Prittlewell Brook, which was my route to the hospital, and the council's proposal would make it extremely dangerous.

In February Amanda had her first chance to appear on television, on the *Look East* programme. I shared my views on the new bus station, the design and location of which were not user friendly.

As Lady wasn't so well now, Alvin and I decided not to go to Majorca and went instead to Eastbourne for a week's holiday. We went by taxi and took both Lady and Amanda with us. This was to be Lady's last visit to Eastbourne.

In April I went to Finland for my EBU meeting.

I began doing my talks again, my first being to the Southend Pensioners, who meet at Avenue Baptist Church in Southend. As I was now 68 years old, I was well qualified to be a member, so I decided to join and would go to meetings when I could. Pensioners' needs are very similar to those of us that are blind and so we can campaign together. We all need better financial benefits and more reliable and frequent bus services.

It was only six days later that the day I'd been dreading for a long time arrived, when my Lady had to be put to sleep.

When Quella was put to sleep we had to take her to the vet's surgery, and I wasn't looking forward to that part. However, this time the vet, Natalie, told me she would come to my house when the time came, and when Lady went off her food that would be the time.

On the morning of 22 May Lady didn't want her breakfast, so I phoned Natalie and she said she would come later on that morning. This gave me time to sit with Lady and Amanda and chat to them both. I sat on the floor, stroking Lady and thanking her for looking after me for 12 years, and telling Amanda that she now had to be a good guide dog and take over from Lady. I'm sure she knew what I was saying, and she responded with lots of licks.

It was very hard for Natalie to put Lady to sleep, as Lady had been her first patient at the Downs practice, when she had removed Lady's tumour the previous year. Natalie was also heavily pregnant. I stayed with Lady to the end and then went out into the garden with Amanda, who comforted me, while Alvin helped Natalie to carry Lady out to the car.

Lady had been a wonderful guide dog and it was so difficult to tell friends and family, who all loved her, that she had died.

Amanda and I went straight to our bungalow at Point Clear for a few days to try to get over the loss. Lady had been Amanda's friend for over two years, and it must be hard for dogs as well as humans to get over the loss of a friend.

In June Alvin, Amanda and I went to Majorca for ten days. It was the first time that Alvin had been in the summer, as we normally went in the winter. Alvin was an albino and due to his lack of skin pigment he could burn easily in the sun. We stayed at the Carla Blanca, as usual, and the staff were very sorry to hear about Lady. Lady had been the first of my guide dogs to go to Majorca when the quarantine regulations changed.

On my return I went to Brussels, where we formed a new committee to look at guide dog training provision and the need for guide dog schools in other countries in Europe. Although the Commission on Mobility and Transport covered guide dog matters, it focused more on access issues rather than the training process. So the European Guide Dog Federation was formed.

Alvin turned 65 in August, and after a party at home we went to stay with my daughter and her family in Rownhams in Hampshire. We all went on a steam railway trip on the Watercress line, just a short distance from Jacqueline's home. Amanda seemed to enjoy the ride. As the gap was quite wide between the platform and the train, a ramp was put out so that she could get aboard safely.

In September it was back to Eastbourne, to the Albany Lions Hotel, for the NFB's Diamond Jubilee conference. As with the Golden Jubilee ten years earlier, I was Conference Secretary. Time seemed to have passed so quickly. Blind and partially sighted people travelled there, mainly by train, from all parts of the UK, together with around 12 dogs, who could be made the scapegoat for any member having a snore during the conference.

In October I returned to Brussels again, this time to take part in a demonstration with other disabled people to encourage the European Parliament to pass legislation to prevent discrimination against those with disabilities.

Later on that month I went to Turkey for the four-yearly EBU General Assembly, and I was pleased to learn that I had been re-elected to chair the Mobility and Transport Commission. As Turkey wouldn't allow guide dogs into the country and none of my friends could go with me for various reasons, I asked Alan from the GDBA if he could find someone to accompany me. I was really surprised when he told me he'd found a man to go with me. Well, Richard turned out to be the perfect guide and he wore his guide dog jacket all day. We were a good advert for guide dogs and we made a lot of contacts in the very large hotel hosting the conference.

People think that when I go to these conferences it's like a holiday, but I can assure you it isn't. This conference started at 8.30 a.m. and finished at 6 p.m. every day, and even during coffee breaks and at lunchtimes there were people to meet and an exhibition to see. However, I do enjoy going to these conferences even though they're very tiring, as you do learn a lot and you get the opportunity to meet many interesting people.

I was brought right back to everyday issues when I got home, when I attended a press conference with my local refuse company, Cory Environmental, who were contracted by Southend Council. For once we had been contacted for our views on how the refuse collections could be improved for blind people. I suggested introducing different kinds of sacks and very soon this system was in place for all residents: a black plain bag for general rubbish, a pink tactile sack for paper and glass, and a white sack with handles for textiles. Amanda enjoyed lying on these sacks for the photo call. The sacks were empty at the time, I hasten to add.

We completed this sad and busy year with a reception at the House of Commons, to campaign for the Higher Rate Mobility Allowance to be extended to blind people.

2008

The first three months of the year were quite routine, with our

Sixties Weekend at Eastbourne and me travelling to Brussels a few times for meetings. St Pancras station had now opened, so the Eurostar trains were now going from there instead of Waterloo. I soon found out that there was a station in Kent called Ebbsfleet, where the Eurostar train stopped. This was only a 45-minute car ride from my house, so from then on I travelled from there to Brussels or Paris. It was so much quicker and cheaper than going by air. Unfortunately, however, they don't have facilities for guide dogs yet at that station, so I still can't take Amanda with me.

In April Alvin had his school reunion in Exeter, Devon. Alvin had six brothers, but due to his poor sight he had to leave his family in the east of London in 1947 and go away to school in Devon. It was quite interesting for me, listening to them all talking about their memories of their school days.

From there we went on to Torquay, where I was due to talk to the local NFB branch, and we stayed with Rose, another guide dog owner. Alvin, Amanda and I spent a day travelling from Torquay on the steam train to Dartmouth and back. Amanda, like most guide dogs, adapts to any place or environment she finds herself in.

After my one-day meeting in Brussels with the Central European Railway Committee, which was a six-monthly event, Amanda and I went off to Scarborough to attend the Annual General Meeting of the Association of Visually-Impaired Office Staff (AVIOS).

For Amanda this was a very special visit, as she had been born in Scarborough in 2003. Breeder Ann Townsend had bred puppies for many years for the GDBA, but she had never seen one of her own pups as a guide dog until now. We were staying at the Delmont Hotel and Amanda got to meet her birth mum,

Kate, and her real grandma, Quiz. Kate was now 10 years old and had retired as a brood bitch, and Quiz was 14 and obviously well retired. Both dogs had produced many pups that had gone on to become guide dogs. It must be hard to see these little bundles of fluff going off at six weeks old, but without people like Ann we just wouldn't have our guide dogs. While I was in the conference Ann took Amanda off for a long run with her mum, followed by a relaxing time at Ann's house with her mum and grandma.

In May we went to Alison and Gordon's villa in Majorca to celebrate Alison's 50th birthday, and all her family had travelled out there for the party, which was held in a venue that staged a pirates show. Gordon had checked with the venue that it was all right for Amanda to go there and, although they'd never had a guide dog before, they said that if she could stand the noise then they had no objections. Well, it certainly was a noisy show, with trapeze artists performing overhead, but Amanda just slept for most of the time under the table, as usual. When we left the staff said they were really surprised at how well Amanda had coped with all the noise. We were there for about three hours, as we'd had a meal as well.

On our return home, Alvin spent a week in hospital. After having a routine examination, he was found to have an infection, and he was back and forth to the hospital all that summer.

Amanda only made a couple of trips to the hospital, unlike Topsy, Quella and Lady, who had taken me there many times to visit my mum, dad and grandma over the years.

Amanda and I returned to Torquay in September for the NFB's annual delegates conference, and then we went on to Bournemouth for the Liberal Democrats conference. We stayed at my daughter's house in Rownhams and travelled to the conference each day on the train.

I finished off this busy month by going on my first cruise. My Uncle Bernard, when he died in 2000, had left me some money. I had been poor all my life but had never got into debt, because we never bought anything we couldn't afford. I knew that Uncle Bernard would want me to enjoy the money and not save it all, so I decided to take a cruise and paid for my friend to come with me. I really enjoyed it and I was so impressed with their use of Braille. Every cabin door had Braille on it, the lifts were talking ones with Braille controls, and the daily bulletin of events was also available in Braille.

With some of Uncle Bernard's money I was also able to buy myself a talking computer.

On returning home I went back to my daughter's for my granddaughter's 13th birthday, for which I'd baked a sponge cake and a fruit cake. With a bag carrying the cakes, plus a case of clothes and a guide dog, I had to depend on staff to help me.

Just a couple of days later I was invited to speak at the first Road Safety Day conference in Paris. It was probably the largest conference I'd ever spoken at, except for the Liberal Democrats conference, where there were normally about 3,000 people. I was speaking about the introduction of shared spaces throughout Europe, which has created 'no go' areas for blind and partially sighted people. In shared spaces the conventional kerb is removed, together with the pedestrian crossings, leaving no safe place for a pedestrian to walk or to cross the road safely. Basically, the driver has to make eye contact with the pedestrian and then you just have to fight for the space. This is obviously no good for blind people, those with learning difficulties or children. At the Paris conference there were 600 delegates from all over Europe, and none of them had considered blind people when designing these shared streets.

I was able to raise the same issue at the International Day of Disabled People in Brussels in December, and also later at a conference in Birmingham, organised by our own Department of Transport.

We only did a couple of local talks this year, but travelling around the country had kept me busy. Amanda was working a lot better and I really felt that she'd become a proper guide dog at last.

2009

On 4 January, the 150th anniversary of the birth of Louis Braille (the inventor of Braille), I was interviewed on BBC Essex and spoke about how important it was for blind people to be taught Braille. I'm not very good at reading it, but I use it every day of my life: for keeping my diary, for reading labels on tins and packets, for setting the regulo on my cooker, for measuring with my tape measure, and for reading my hymn books and Bible. Unfortunately, nowadays there are very few people teaching Braille, so those going blind have little opportunity to learn it.

Our annual Sixties Weekend had become increasingly popular and was fully booked. So far we'd been lucky with weather, always just missing the snow and ice.

On 27 January I was appointed as a trustee of Disability Essex, based in Rochford. I took on this job as I wanted to cut down on my travelling to London and beyond and thought that working in Essex would involve a much easier journey for a soon-to-be 69-year-old.

In February I attended the memorial service for Sir John Wall, CBE, who had died the previous November. John had been the Chairman of the RNIB for many years and President of the EBU for some time as well. It was John who had asked me in 1988 to represent the RNIB at that first women's conference, and he'd also nominated me to chair the Commission on Mobility and Guide Dogs. He was a great comfort the previous year when Alvin was in hospital, as he'd suffered with the same problem himself. The service in London was packed with blind people and John's family and friends from all parts of the world. Although John didn't have a guide dog, he had always supported us, and there were many dogs at the service.

My 69th birthday was spent in London at the Natural History Museum, which was celebrating Louis Braille's birthday. David Blunkett hosted this event as patron of the RNIB. I followed this with a two-day meeting in Brussels, where a two-year project was launched to assess the transport needs of people over the age of 50.

In April we celebrated the 80th birthday of one of our friends, Barbara, who had taken my retired guide dogs for many walks over the years.

May was a busy month. We had our regular EBU meeting, at the Travel Inn in London, which provided accommodation for our European members. On this occasion my friend Barbara came as well. On our return journey she phoned her usual taxi company, a different one to the one I used, and booked a cab to meet us at Chalkwell station.

When we arrived at the station, a member of staff took us to the car and Barbara carried our cases to the boot for the driver to load. As usual, I got in the front seat with Amanda and she curled up at my feet. On seeing Amanda, the driver stated quite categorically, "I do not take dogs!" I told him that it was illegal for him to refuse me, which he obviously knew, so he had no option but to take us. I spent most of the journey back to my house trying to explain to the taxi driver why he should accept guide dogs. The driver dropped off Amanda and me at our house and then took Barbara to hers. The driver said he would have to go home and wash himself now, so I reported him to the Council, who issued him with a warning letter stating that if he refused another guide dog he would lose his licence. Some drivers avoid taking guide dogs by not responding to calls from known guide dog owners' houses.

On 14 May the first demonstration against shared streets in Kensington High Street took place, and this was shown on London television that night.

On 22 May it was the second anniversary of losing Lady and I was still missing her, and the following day marked exactly 20 years since Moira had first started to come and help me. Moira comes most Monday mornings and reads the post, writes birthday and thank you cards and just helps me with any reading I need doing. She reads from catalogues, as few of them are produced on tape. Like Barbara, Moira walked all my retired dogs and even looked after them when I went abroad for day meetings. She also sews special colour buttons onto my clothes so that I know what colour I'm wearing. This colour coding was invented by John Slade.

From the time that the NFB launched the 'Give Us Back Our Pavement' campaign back in 1978, 6 June had always been known as Pavement Day, although the name held a different meaning now, with the introduction of the shared streets schemes.

We arranged the second demonstration in Ashford in Kent, where the high street had been turned into a shared street, thus ignoring the needs of blind and partially sighted people. This demonstration was filmed by BBC Television, and NFB members came from as far away as Yorkshire to show their support.

This was followed by a lunch at the House of Commons organised by the GDBA, to educate the Members of Parliament in terms of the dangers of shared streets, where guide dogs have no kerb to stop at and no pedestrian crossing to use to take us safely through moving traffic.

In August I was invited to talk to the Chelmsford Access Committee about shared streets. Chelmsford Council had plans to install a shared street in the town, but after a lot of lobbying this scheme was abandoned.

I had been writing my autobiography for five years now, but I hadn't been able to secure a publisher. I'd sent three chapters to three different publishers but without any luck. Then one afternoon I was listening to BBC Essex and Steve Scruton was talking to an author who said his book had been published by a local publisher called Apex, based in Clacton, where my bungalow is. So I phoned Directory Enquiries and they found the number for me.

When I telephoned Apex Chris Cowlin answered the phone, and after speaking to him I sent him some chapters, after which he offered me a contract. So, on 7 September, I signed the contract for my book to be published the following July. Chris wanted me to write some more chapters, which I did, and I finally finished the book while on holiday in Majorca in November. Chris said he would have the book ready for my 70th birthday the following March.

Even though I was busy writing additional material for the book, I had to carry on going to meetings. The second mediate meeting of the two-year project took place in Germany and The Lib Dem conference was held in Bournemouth for the second year running. Then followed a conference in Birmingham run by the

GDBA, looking at all the mobility and transport needs of blind people.

On 10 October it was the 50th anniversary of the Ladies' Club at my church, so we held a special service and then had a meal out to celebrate. We meet on alternate Monday evenings in the church hall and I try to go as often as I can, as it gives me a break from all my other voluntary work. It only takes me three minutes to get to the church. When I first started to go there with Lady, as the floors were hard one of the ladies provided a mat for her to lie on, and this became a regular routine whether in the church, church hall or out on a coffee morning or for lunch. Now the mat is brought out for Amanda.

A week later I met Chris Cowlin for the first time, when he came to see me at Point Clear to discuss which photograph would be suitable for the front and back covers of my new book. I was thrilled to bits when he chose the picture of me receiving my MBE in 1983 with my third guide dog, Brandy for the front cover. For the back he chose a picture of me at my 21st birthday party, cutting the cake I'd made. Chris also asked me for some suggestions for a title, so I sent him a list, and he chose Alvin's idea of 'Just Jill'.

On 1 November we were allowed to fly for the first time from Stansted airport to Palma with Amanda, via EasyJet. It was so much easier than going to Heathrow. We'd been to Stansted the previous year to train the staff in regard to the Passports for Pets scheme. A chip has been inserted into Amanda's shoulder, so all the staff were testing their equipment on her, which she didn't mind at all. In fact, she really enjoyed all the attention.

On our return from Majorca I completed the book and Peter checked it for me before submitting it for editing.

On 1 and 2 December I attended another road safety

conference in Brussels and came home for the International Day of Disabled People, to speak at a one-day event in Chelmsford, organised by the Chelmsford Access Committee.

It was at this event that I first met Sue Parker, who was working for Disability Essex, for which I was a trustee. Sue drove me home from a meeting one day, and we have remained friends ever since. She has taken over the role of my guide on my trips abroad, when I can't take Amanda, as Barbara and Moira, who accompanied me on so many trips, are older than me and now find the travelling very tiring and difficult, whereas Sue is a lot younger.

2010

The year started with me talking to the Essex Planning Group of People with Sensory Disabilities at Chelmsford, mainly about my work in Europe and for the NFB, and this was followed by our Sixties Weekend at Eastbourne, despite very bad weather.

My book had been edited and Moira started to read it to me so that I could make any corrections required. Jacqueline came to finish this process, and I received the final copy on 9 March, just one day before my 70th birthday.

My birthday party was held on 6 March in Chalkwell Park Rooms, just a few minutes' walk from my home and in the park where all my guide dogs have enjoyed most of their free runs. The only other guide dog that came to my party was that of Mr Jim Downs, who was the vet for most of my guide dogs before he went blind himself. I had a lovely party with 63 friends and family present.

It just so happened that on my birthday the GDBA had arranged a reception about talking buses at the House of Commons and I was invited to attend. So, with my book in my bag and Amanda by my side, off we went on our own to celebrate my birthday. Sue Sharp and her husband had taken pictures at my party four days earlier, and I had a lovely surprise when Sue presented me with a photograph album containing all the photos. She had written by hand, in Braille, descriptions for each photo, and I was so pleased with such a kind thought from Sue.

When I returned home we went for a meal at our favourite restaurant, Spaghetti Junction, which is only five minutes' walk away from our house.

A week later Amanda and I had a very early start, as we were the guests on the Ray Clark show on BBC Essex. We had to arrive at 6 a.m. and we were on the programme until 9 a.m. Ray talked to me about my life and my book, while Amanda sat quietly under the table throughout.

On 27 June my church, Chalkwell Park Methodist, held a service to bless my new book. I chose the hymns and Peter came to read one of the lessons from Braille. Eve, the chairlady of our Ladies' Club, whom I'd known for 40 years, read the other lesson. Amanda was quite surprised to sit in the front row, as she was used to sitting on Lady's mat in our normal spot a few rows back.

On 27 June it was the anniversary of my dad's death in 1978, so he was very much in my thoughts that day. He had been a member of the Methodist Church all his life: the first 27 years at Enfield Methodist, where he was christened and got married to my mum in 1937; and then at Benfleet Methodist from 1937 until his death in 1978. He was also a scoutmaster and trustee of the Church. He would have been so proud of me.

The following day I was off to France for the second time this year, for a meeting with Nissan Cars in order to test the new silent electric car. Blind people, whilst appreciating the need to cut the levels of pollution, are concerned about the quietness of the vehicle. I have good hearing, but even in the quiet testing area I had a real problem hearing the vehicles passing me. The project is continuing and they are planning to put a sound onto each electric vehicle.

July must've been one of my busiest months for years. It started on 1 July with Amanda and I going to Loughborough University for a two-day training course for the Appeals Service. I was then doing interviews on the radio about my book every day from home.

I then had three days at Point Clear prior to the book launch on 16 July, which was held at Porters, the Civic House of Southend. The Mayor of Southend, Councillor Ann Holland, hosted this for me. On the following day we did our first book signing at Lakeside Shopping Centre. Amanda really enjoys these, as everyone wants to make a fuss of her.

In order to sign my book I've had to learn to write again. This wasn't easy, as I hadn't written words since losing my sight in 1964. Although I could sign my name, over the previous 18 years I'd used a signature stamp, which enabled me to sign my name automatically on cheques, etc.

My first talk on the subject of my book was at my church's Ladies' Club on the Monday.

Just three days later I went to the RNIB to receive a Lifetime Achievers award. This was the first time that this award had been given.

We went straight from there to be filmed for the *Times* web page, about access for guide dogs. The interview was with Ron Liddle.

The following day I went to a reunion at my old school, King John's at Benfleet. This was the first time I'd attended one and it was just by chance that I'd heard about it on the radio. The phone number that was given out on BBC Essex turned out to be that of Ann Adams, who turned out to be an old playmate from when I lived in Benfleet as a little girl. Ann is now one of my friends and she helps me a lot.

The last day of this busy month was Monty Martin's birthday. Monty is one of the Appeals Service judges, with whom I'd sat on the panel for 18 years. He is also one of Amanda's favourite men, and she would always try to sit on his feet while at a tribunal and expected a quick walk at lunchtime to spend a penny. So Amanda was very pleased to be invited to his special birthday party, which was held in a Chinese restaurant.

On 19 August I was a guest on the Michael Ball television show. My publisher had arranged this, and Michael Ball talked to me about my book and, of course, Amanda. When we were rehearsing, the cameraman said to Amanda, "Just look at me." Amanda, who loves men, did just that. So, you might say, Amanda was the star of the show. Not even the smell of the curry that Michael cooked for me as part of the programme turned her head from that cameraman.

August was nearly as busy as July. We went to York and Scarborough for book signings, and also to celebrate Alvin's birthday. Alvin loves steam trains, so while I was signing books Alvin and our friend Barbara were off on a steam train for the day. It also gave Amanda another chance to see her real mother, and Ann took Amanda and Kate off for a nice free run. I'm sure Amanda needed it after her busy month of working.

The following week Amanda and I went to Eastbourne to attend a charity event organised by Mr Gulzart, the manager of the Albany Lions Hotel, where we hold our Sixties Weekends.

Over the bank holiday weekend I took my daughter Jacqueline

on a four-day cruise to Cork in Ireland. It was very easy, as Jacqueline lives near Southampton, the cruise ship's starting point.

On my return I went to Brussels for three days of meetings, and then came back to be filmed by a French company that was making a film about blind people living in the UK. Amanda is very good with filming. We have to walk backwards and forwards so many times, and she is always looking at the camera.

On the following day was the opening of Disability Essex's new building, which is the first eco-friendly, fully accessible building in the country.

Amanda celebrated her seventh birthday at the BBC's Broadcasting House in London. We'd gone there to record for the *In Touch* programme. Peter White interviewed me about my book, and when it was broadcast it took up the whole programme. It was also repeated on *You and Yours* on Radio 4 a couple of weeks later.

The first two weeks of November were spent in Majorca, where we were very lucky with hot weather.

Jacqueline travelled up from her home in Hampshire one evening so that she could take me Christmas shopping in Southend the following day, and we parked up in Debenhams' car park at around 9.30 a.m. We had a lovely day's shopping, but when we returned to the car park we were charged £15, as we were 15 minutes over the 7 hours. This made me quite cross. However, on the way home I telephoned my husband Alvin, who was still working in his music shop, just to let him know that we were heading back. He told me that a letter had arrived for me from the Prime Minister, but his sight wasn't good enough to read ordinary print so he couldn't see what it was about. He thought it was something to do with a new committee.

Jacqueline and I arrived home and, after feeding Amanda and putting the kettle on, Jacqueline looked at the letter. She then said, "Mum, you'd better sit down." She read it to me, and it informed me that I was going to be given an OBE in the New Year's Honours. The letter stipulated that it was confidential and I mustn't tell anyone. We did read the letter to Alvin, but no one else knew until 1 January.

Each year I write a newsletter to enclose with our Christmas cards, to let friends and relatives know what Alvin and I have been doing during the year, and also to let people know how Jacqueline, Mike and my two grandchildren, Joseph and Emily, are getting on with their lives, but I'd already written the 2010 newsletter when I received this notification. We decided to tell the grandchildren on 31 December, as this was the day that the press would phone to do their pre-recorded interviews.

In the past I'd had a party at Christmas to thank the people that had helped us during the year, but I hadn't organised one for a couple of years. So I decided to arrange one for 1 January, although I didn't tell anyone what it was really for.

Most of December was spent indoors, as we had heavy snow and ice. Alvin had to take Amanda for a walk each day, as it was too dangerous for me to go out.

My meeting in Brussels was cancelled and we couldn't do our annual collection for the NFB in the high street.

2011

It was during the party on 1 January, when Amanda was lying on her back in the middle of the room inviting strokes, as usual, that my friends noticed she had a little lump on her tummy. I'd felt it myself a few weeks earlier but, as it was so small and it didn't appear to be causing her any pain, I didn't do anything about it.

However, now that my friends had mentioned it, I decided I should take her to the vet the next day. It did spoil my party a little, as it reminded me of Topsy's and Lady's lumps, and Amanda was so young.

The vet, Margaret, whom I'd known for many years, thought it was just a fleshy lump but decided that it ought to be removed, as it was just where the buckle of her harness fastened.

I'd already arranged to give a talk on 11 January at Hadleigh United Reformed Church, the day the vet chose for the operation, and as I didn't want to let the church down I decided to go ahead with it. We took Amanda to the vet's in the morning and left her there for her operation.

I was in my kitchen all by myself later on in the morning when my phone rang. It was one of the vets, a man I didn't know, who said that he had just opened up Amanda and had found two lumps. He wanted my permission to remove them both. Straight away I said, "Yes, if you agree."

Vera picked me up at 2 p.m. and took me to my talk. Everyone was so disappointed not to see Amanda but understood why she wasn't there. I had to leave my mobile phone switched on throughout the talk so that the vet's could contact me. They rang to say that Amanda was ready to be picked, and Vera took me to collect her on the way home.

The lumps were tested and they were, as Margaret had thought, just fatty lumps. Although Amanda recovered quite quickly from the operation, as the wound was just beneath the position of her harness buckle my trainer suggested that we didn't let her work for a month until it had healed.

Two days after Amanda's operation I travelled to Eastbourne by car for the Sixties Weekend, but Alvin was able to guide me. I'd been to the Albany Lions Hotel so many times that I knew my way around it anyway.

Although Amanda wasn't allowed any long walks, it all turned out all right, and she was soon back to her lively self and once again outrunning all the other dogs in the park. It was a very worrying time for me, as she was only seven years old.

I was awaiting my invitation to Buckingham Palace to receive my OBE and I wanted Amanda to be fit to accompany me. Of course, the big question was: would she be allowed in? I also needed a new suit for the presentation, and my new friend Ann, whom I'd met the previous year at my school reunion, offered to take me to the January sales at Lakeside Shopping Centre. I bought a dress and jacket in turquoise blue. This was just prior to our trip to Eastbourne, and while I was there I was able to find a hat to match and also bought some ribbon of the same colour so that Amanda could have a matching bow. All I wanted then was the date to attend.

My previous visit to the Palace to receive my MBE back in 1983 had been on 10 February, but I received a letter notifying me that this time the presentation would be on 31 March. I was also required to complete a form, giving the names of the three people that would be accompanying me. On the previous occasion I could only take two people with me, so it was an easy decision - my first husband, Mick, and my daughter, Jacqueline, then 19 years old.

As my husband Alvin had an eye operation booked for that day and had also been to be Palace before, having won a ticket for a garden party there, I thought perhaps I should take my daughter and my two grandchildren. However, my grandson Joseph had been ill and was in the middle of his A-levels at college, so he didn't want to take any more time off. In the end, Alvin asked for his operation to be moved and he was given a new date in August, so he was able to come to the Palace with me, together with Jacqueline and my granddaughter Emily, now 15 years old.

Another form that I had to fill in asked if I had a disability, so I said I was totally blind and I would be accompanied by my guide dog, Amanda, a black Labrador.

Within a week of returning the forms I received a reply informing me that I should go to a different entrance door than previously advised. I telephoned St James's Palace to find out why and was told this was so that I could meet up with the page, who would be escorting me. I said that last time my guide dog Brandy hadn't been allowed to stay with me, but I was told it had been sanctioned that Amanda could stay with me throughout the ceremony. Obviously I was very pleased to hear this, as not having my guide dog with me on the previous occasion had marred the day for me. In fact, Amanda was the first guide dog to be allowed into an investiture.

On 1 January, when my OBE was announced, I was interviewed on BBC Essex, first on the news, then on Etholle's morning show, and later that morning on Timbo's show.

Well, Timbo started to joke with me that he wanted to go to Buckingham Palace, and after much banter on the programme between us it was agreed that Timbo would take me in his car to the Palace. He got one of his listeners to lend him a chauffeur's hat and another to arrange for the congestion charge to be waived, and another lady lent me a hatpin.

Jacqueline and Emily travelled up the night before and stayed in a hotel near Waterloo, and had arranged to meet us outside the Palace.

It was 31 March 2011. My hairdresser Edna had come to do my hair the night before, so we were all ready for the big day. The alarm was set for 5 a.m., so that I could get up and feed Amanda. Normally, I wouldn't feed her prior to a car journey, but I was unsure how long it would take and didn't want to be worrying about feeding her at the Palace.

BBC Essex had arranged to arrive at 6.15 a.m. to interview me, and programme presenter Ray Clark's first words when his show started at 6 a.m. were, "Good morning everyone. I hope you're all well dressed, as we're off to Buckingham Palace today."

Timbo arrived with Felicity and started recording at 6.25 a.m. I'd been led to believe that Timbo had an old banger but, oh no, it was a black Mercedes. I sat in the front, with Amanda curled up at my feet, and Alvin sat in the back.

We left at 7 a.m. and didn't arrive at the Palace until 9.50 a.m. We were due there at 10 a.m., so we only just made it in time. The traffic was really heavy and we were all getting a bit worried that we'd be late. We had to stop outside the Palace so that our car could be checked by the police, so while this was happening Alvin took Amanda across the road to Green Park to spend a penny. Jacqueline and Emily joined us at this point and climbed into the back of the car.

When Alvin arrived back with Amanda, as she got back into the car the police asked if she was a bomb dog! I replied, "No, she's my guide dog." So we were given the all-clear and off we drove through the Palace gates.

I was met by the Palace staff, who escorted us all inside. After we'd all taken the opportunity to go to the toilet, Alvin and Emily were taken to their seats in the ballroom. Jacqueline was able to stay with me right up until the ceremony started, at 11 a.m., and I was in the queue. Mark, the page, stayed alongside me throughout.

That day 101 people were receiving awards and Her Royal

Highness Princess Anne was making the presentations.

When I arrived in front of Princess Anne she stepped down from her rostrum so that she was on the same level as me. Amanda lay down and didn't get up until we'd finished speaking, which must've been after about 5 minutes. Princess Anne hooked my medal onto the clip that had been fastened on to me and, after shaking hands, I did my curtsy and we walked away.

In a separate room the medal was removed and placed in a box for me to take home. I then went and sat with Jacqueline, Emily and Alvin.

The ceremony finished at 1 p.m. and, as we left, a video was taken of us, together with all the photographs that we'd ordered and paid for in advance of the day. I'd booked for us all to have tea at the Dorchester Hotel following the ceremony and, thinking that it would be over by 12.15 p.m., which is the usual time when the Queen is doing the presentations, I'd booked for 1.15 p.m. When I spoke to the staff at the hotel they told me not to worry and extended our time. We arrived there at about 2 p.m.

When we left the Palace, Sue Sharp and her husband met us to take some photos and then joined us for tea at the Dorchester. We were held up by the Prime Minister of Turkey, who arrived at the Dorchester at the same time as us. We'd all walked in thinking that we were more important than their party. It was a lovely atmosphere, with music playing and a lovely scent in the air from all the flower displays.

While we were having our tea, Timbo phoned the Steve Scruton show and once again I was on live, telling Steve all about the day. We left after two hours, having really enjoyed our tea, and we were given two boxes of cakes to take home.

Sue took Amanda to the toilet while we waited for the staff to bring Timbo's car back round to the front door. This time we were ahead of the Prime Minister of Turkey.

When Sue got back she told me that Amanda had done a 'big packet'. "Do you think it would be all right to give it to the doorman?" she asked. As there didn't seem to be any bins around, we did just that.

The doorman, most politely, said, "Of course, madam. I will get rid of it for you."

We just couldn't stop laughing.

We arrived home at about 7 p.m. I felt very tired but so very happy after a day I will never forget.

A few friends came round in the evening and we had some champagne and the cakes from the Dorchester. Amanda was still awake enough to pick up the crumbs and, of course, to ensure that a lot of fuss was made of her.

Getting back to this year's Sixties Weekend in Eastbourne, we had a full hotel of 95 blind and partially sighted people, together with 12 guide dogs. This year we also had two guide dog puppies, which were being puppy walked by my friends Lyn and Jenny.

I'd met Lyn at Point Clear, where she had a holiday bungalow, like me. She'd become a puppy walker a couple of years earlier and, as I'd only ever met the puppy walkers of my own guide dogs after I'd qualified, it was really nice to meet a puppy walker while the puppy was still a pup. I can remember Lyn coming to see me the day after her first puppy had gone off for training. She was so upset and couldn't speak. I just said to her, "Just think, without you a blind person wouldn't be able to have a guide dog."

Puppy walkers are volunteers who look after guide dog puppies from the age of six weeks, until they go for training at about ten months old. The puppy walker does do a certain amount of training with the puppy, such as house training, going to the toilet in a designated area, stopping at steps, and getting them used to travelling on buses and trains and also walking round supermarkets and shopping centres. Some will be taken to a church and to the theatre, and Lyn, who currently has an eight-week-old puppy, has just taken him to a brass band concert. Coming to our Sixties Weekend gets them used to being with other dogs and being in a hotel environment. It is just a case of getting them used to the life they'll have when they're guide dogs.

I advertise the Sixties Weekends on a monthly tape magazine that I've produced for five years, called *Mobility Matters*, on behalf of the charity, Living Without Sight. These tapes go out each month to about 800 blind people, many of whom are guide dog owners. It is interesting to hear different points of view on all sorts of mobility and transport issues. Usually, around 15 people contribute to the tape each month. It's really sad when we hear that a member's dog has died, but it's also exciting to hear when the newly trained guide dog arrives. We can exchange information between one another; for instance, in the bad winter we passed on details of shoe chains that could be bought to wear in the snow and ice. Alvin got a supply of yellow safety jackets from the Pound Shop so that we could be seen more clearly by the traffic.

On 25 January Amanda and I took part in some research for *Which?* magazine. We had to be undercover passengers on a flight between Gatwick and Manchester airports. We stayed overnight and then flew back the next day. Our findings featured in the April edition of the *Which? Travel* magazine and certainly revealed a need for staff training in understanding the needs of people with disabilities.

On 1 February it was the 58th anniversary of the Canvey floods and I attended the unveiling of a new plaque. It listed the names of all the people that drowned in the floods, which included my auntie and uncle, Eddie and Will White. With me was my friend Cynthia, with whom I'd shared a ward in Southend Hospital when I went totally blind. Cynthia was only 14 years old at the time and she helped me to get around the ward and took me to the toilet. I called her my first guide dog. Cynthia eventually had to have both her eyes removed, and we have supported each other through difficult times in our lives.

At the memorial service, taken by the vicar of Cynthia's Canvey Island church, our two guide dogs, Una and Amanda, sat side by side listening to the very moving tributes.

A few days later Alvin, Amanda and I travelled to Scarborough for a Sixties Weekend organised by the Delmont Hotel. This gave Amanda another chance to see her real mum, Kate, now 14 years old, but her grandma, Quiz, had now died.

Most of March was spent doing routine things, such as sitting on appeals and attending meetings.

My 71st birthday was a little quieter than the previous year. I went shopping in Southend with Sue and then had a meal out with my family and friends.

At the end of April Alvin and I went on a four-day cruise from Southampton to Cobh in Ireland. It was Alvin's first cruise, and it was nice as we were able to spend a lot of time dancing, my favourite hobby. I was also able to give a talk to guests one morning. Sixty people turned up, and I was able to sell 20 copies of my book. Amanda stayed with our friends, Carol and Stewart, at Gidea Park. Carol had been Fabian's puppy walker and had often looked after our guide dogs when we couldn't take them abroad with us.

On my return I gave two talks, both to groups that I'd spoken to back in the 1970s: Thorpe Bay Methodist and Rayleigh Townswomen's Guild.

On 8 June I did a very special talk at my local library in Westcliff. It was this library that had sparked my access campaigning back in November 1971, the day after I'd qualified as a guide dog owner with Topsy, when I was asked to leave. This time I was invited to go and speak about my book and I was made very welcome. I hope to be going to other libraries in the area.

Later on in the month we went to a conference at Stansted, where I spoke about shared streets. I was able to tell the conference that, as a result of proper consultation between Chelmsford Council and the local Access Committee, we were able to stop a shared space scheme from being introduced. Unfortunately, we heard of another shared space that was being planned for Hadleigh, a nearby district.

It was only 11 days later that I returned to talk to the Hadleigh Church group, where I'd been in January while Amanda was having her operation. Most of the members, all residents of Hadleigh, weren't aware of this proposed scheme. They were very pleased to see that Amanda had recovered completely from her operation and was fit and well.

Southend Council, unlike Chelmsford Council, failed to take on board our concerns and introduced two shared areas on 1 April, one outside our main Victoria railway station and one at City Beach. Ever since, I've been campaigning against these dangerous shared spaces and launched a petition in July on behalf of the Southend Pensioners and our local NFB branch. On 23 July I took part in a demonstration, alongside other residents, at City Beach, to highlight the danger of such shared spaces for blind people, who rely on their guide dogs to stop at a kerb or a pedestrian crossing in order to ensure their safe mobility.

August was a mixed month of emotions for me. Our bungalow at Point Clear had to be demolished due to subsidence, and we spent a whole day clearing out the contents ready for its demolition. However, on 18 August came the really good news that my grandson Joseph, now 18, despite suffering health problems since the previous October, had passed his A-level exams and had qualified for a place at Bristol University.

I was very honoured to have Joseph accompany me to lunch at the House of Lords with Lord Low of Dalston. We then listened to the Welfare Reform debate in the chamber, which was very relevant to another current campaign, relating to the replacement of the Disability Living Allowance with the Personal Independence Payment scheme. Amanda and I attended two meetings on this subject in September, travelling to London.

On 27 September Amanda was very confused when we visited Point Clear to see our new bungalow being built. All that was left of the old bungalow was the gate and the front wall. I think she really wondered where her food, bed and toys had gone. I'm sure she'll be much happier when it's completely finished and we'll be able to return once again for our long walks along the coast, with lovely fresh air and sea breezes.

The GDBA is soon to celebrate its 80th birthday, from 1 to 8 October. This will be a very special week for all guide dog owners and their supporters.

For me it will also be a memorable week for other reasons, as Joseph will be travelling to his university on 2 October, and on 4 October I will be taking part in the 50th anniversary celebrations of the Radio 4 *In Touch* programme, with which I've been associated since 1968, contributing on many issues relating to blindness. Then on 6 October my granddaughter Emily will be celebrating her 16th birthday, followed by a special service at Lawfords Parish Church on 9 October to celebrate the 80th anniversary of the GDBA.

It is 11 November as I conclude my 40-year journey as a guide dog owner, and I wish to pay tribute to my past five guide dogs - Topsy, Bunty, Brandy, Quella and Lady - as well as my current guide dog, Amanda, who will by then be eight years old, for all the love and affection they have shown me and, most importantly of all, for keeping me safe and giving me the confidence I needed in order to carry out all the voluntary work I have done over these past 40 years, both locally and nationally.